SHOW WHAT YOU KNOW

OAT

For Grade 4

grade 4

PREPARATION FOR THE
OHIO ACHIEVEMENT TESTS

NAME

Published by:
Show What You Know® Publishing
A Division of Englefield & Associates, Inc.
P.O. Box 341348
Columbus, OH 43234-1348
Phone: 614-764-1211
www.showwhatyouknowpublishing.com
www.passtheoat.com

Copyright © 2004 by Englefield & Associates, Inc.

All rights reserved. No part of this book, including interior design, cover design, and icons, may be reproduced or transmitted in any form, by any means (electronic, photocopying, recording, or otherwise), without the prior written permission of the publisher.

Printed in the United States of America
06 05   19 18 17 16 15 14 13 12 11 10 9 8 7 6 5 4 3

ISBN: 1-59230-071-5

Limit of Liability/Disclaimer of Warranty: The authors and publishers have used their best efforts in preparing this book. Englefield & Associates, Inc., and the authors make no representations or warranties with respect to the contents of this book and specifically disclaim any implied warranties and shall in no event be liable for any loss of any kind including but not limited to special, incidental, consequential, or other damages.

Acknowledgements

Show What You Know® Publishing acknowledges the following for their efforts in making this assessment material available for Ohio students, parents, and teachers.

Cindi Englefield, President/Publisher
Eloise Boehm-Sasala, Vice President/Managing Editor
Lainie Burke, Project Editor/Graphic Designer
Erin Richers, Project Editor
Rob Ciccotelli, Project Editor
Christine Filippetti, Project Editor
Jennifer Harney, Illustrator/Cover Designer

About the Contributors

The content of this book was written BY teachers FOR teachers and students and was designed specifically for the Ohio Achievement Test (OAT) for Grade 4. Contributions to the Writing, Reading, and Mathematics sections of this book were also made by the educational publishing staff at Show What You Know® Publishing. Dr. Jolie S. Brams, a clinical child and family psychologist, is the contributing author of the Test Anxiety and Test-Taking Strategies chapters of this book. Without the contributions of these people, this book would not be possible.

Table of Contents

Introduction vi

Test Anxiety 1

Test-Taking Strategies 9

Writing 21
    Introduction 21
    Questions I Will Answer on the OAT 22
    Item Distribution on the OAT for Grade 4 Writing 23
    Scoring 23
    Directions for Practice Test 1 25
    Practice Test 1 26
    Directions for Practice Test 2 38
    Practice Test 2 39

Reading 51
    Introduction 51
    Questions I Will Answer on the OAT 52
    Item Distribution on the OAT for Grade 4 Reading 53
    Scoring 53
    Directions for Practice Test 1 55
    Practice Test 1 56
    Directions for Practice Test 2 71
    Practice Test 2 72

Mathematics 87
    Introduction 87
    Questions I Will Answer on the OAT 88
    Item Distribution on the OAT for Grade 4 Mathematics 89
    Scoring 89
    Directions for Practice Test 1 91
    Practice Test 1 92
    Directions for Practice Test 2 106
    Practice Test 2 107

Introduction

The purpose of the Ohio Achievement Test (OAT) is to measure student learning. Throughout the school year, students are exposed to a wide variety of concepts from a range of disciplines, only some of which are tested by the OAT. Yet it is important that all Ohio Academic Content Standards be taught in order to ensure that students have a well-rounded understanding of the fourth-grade curriculum. Students who have been taught the elements of the Ohio Academic Content Standards curriculum will have been exposed to all that is assessed by the OAT. Nonetheless, students will benefit from the review of key details as they prepare to take this assessment.

The *Show What You Know® on the OAT for Grade 4, Practice Test Workbook* is designed to help students better understand the types of information they will see on the OAT. This book will help students review important elements assessed by the OAT; it is not a substitute for continuous teaching and learning, which take place both in and outside the classroom. But, as with any assessment, it is a good idea to review principles that have been taught and learned prior to taking the OAT.

Show What You Know® on the OAT for Grade 4, Practice Test Workbook includes many features that will benefit students as they prepare for the OAT.

The first two chapters—Test Anxiety and Test-Taking Strategies—were written especially for fourth graders. Test Anxiety offers advice on how to reduce anxious feelings about tests, and Test-Taking Strategies gives strategies students can use to do their best on tests.

The Writing, Reading, and Mathematics chapters of this book will introduce students to the types of questions they will answer on the OAT. In addition, there are two practice tests per subject. These tests will help students become familiar with the look and feel of the OAT. Each practice test is a great opportunity for students to practice their test-taking skills.

For easy reference, this Practice Test Workbook correlates with the *Show What You Know® on the OAT for Grade 4, Parent/Teacher Supplement* (sold separately).

Test Anxiety

Introduction

Most fourth graders can think of many activities that are more fun than taking a test like the Ohio Achievement Test (OAT) for Grade 4! If you were asked, "What would you rather do? Go to recess? See a movie? Eat a snack? Go swimming? Take a test?" you would almost NEVER choose to take a test. This does not mean that you are afraid to take tests; it just means that you like to have fun!

Sometimes, students do not like tests for another BIG reason. Even though they may be able to do well, they are afraid of tests and afraid of failing. This fear happens to all of us some of the time and to some of us all of the time. If you are ever worried about tests, you are not alone!

This section of the book contains 11 "STRESS BUSTER" exercises. Stress is the uncomfortable feeling you have when your thoughts get in the way of doing your best and showing what you know. When grown-ups and kids feel stress, they feel rotten! The "STRESS BUSTERS" were written to help you feel calm, happy, proud, and in control.

If your mind is a mess
Because of terrible stress,
And you feel that you can't change at all,
Just pick up this book
And take a look.
STRESS BUSTERS won't let you fall!

Stress Buster One: A Test Is Only a Challenge

Just hearing the word "test" can be scary. This is because some students often think of "test" and "failure" at the same time. But tests are not made for you to fail! Tests are made to push you to learn as much as you can and do the best that you can do. The OAT was made to let you "show what you know." The test is a CHALLENGE for you.

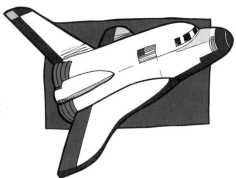

A challenge is simply a goal that is not easy to reach. One of the space shuttles was named "Challenger" because each of its missions made important scientific and space discoveries that were difficult to complete. Each mission was a "challenge." Think of your favorite football team; the quarterback is hurt, and, next week, the team is playing its toughest rival. Your mom says, "Next week's game will be a test!" What she means is, "Next week's game will be a challenge–difficult but not impossible." A test is just a challenge.

Stress Buster Two: Your "Alarm" System

You may think that the only alarms are fire alarms or burglar alarms, but humans have a special "alarm," too. This alarm helps you in dangerous situations by letting you know that you should pay attention. When something seems dangerous, your mind and your body become "alarmed." You may not hear a bell or buzzer go off, but your heart jumps, and you can't think of anything but the problem. Usually, this alarm is helpful in saving you from being hurt, but, sometimes, this alarm can signal at the wrong times, such as when you have to take a test.

One way to become less alarmed when facing a test is to understand how you feel when that alarm goes off. Close your eyes and picture yourself taking a walk in your neighborhood or in a park near your house. You are walking and looking at the deep, green grass and trees on a warm summer day. The flowers are in bloom, and you can smell the sweet nectar and hear the bees buzzing. Suddenly, a large, barking dog jumps out in front of you from behind the bushes. Write down how you think you might feel when the dog jumps out. How would your face look? What would your body do?

_____

_____

_____

Stress Buster Three: Learning to Be Courageous by Practicing

What do you need to know to be a police officer? Most kids would laugh at this question; to be a police officer, you need to know the law. While this is true, police officers need to learn much more than just how to uphold the law. They must go through training to learn how to chase a criminal on foot or in a cruiser, what to do during a robbery, and how to help citizens in an emergency. Police officers must use their knowledge and their common sense. They have to learn to control their fear. Even police officers have fears and worries! Police officers feel stress, too!

Police officers win over worry and fear in many ways. They practice over and over until they have mastered their skills. They pretend to be in all kinds of threatening situations so they know how to handle those situations successfully. They learn how to protect themselves and others. Police officers also have to go through training about controlling their fears. When faced with certain emergencies, they have to "talk to themselves" to calm themselves down. They learn to tell themselves they can do a good job and not to think of the worst that can happen. They tell themselves that it is OK to be a little nervous, but not terribly nervous. They remind themselves that they have had a lot of practice and can probably get out of this difficult situation.

What can you learn from this? To practice what you know. The more you practice, the braver you will be!

Stress Buster Four: Do You Know Who This Is? Someone Who Never Gave Up!

You will feel better about tests and feel less stressed when you remember that many people, even famous people, failed many times before they succeeded. When something is hard for you, keep going! If you give up, you will feel like you can only fail. That will make you even MORE STRESSED!

Look what happened in the life of this famous person!

- He did not read until he was nine.
- He failed in business when he was 22.
- He lost a race for the legislature at age 23.
- His business failed again when he was 24.
- He became very physically ill when he was 27.
- He lost a race for Congress when he was 34.
- He lost again at age 39.
- He tried to run for Senate when he was 45 but lost.
- He tried to become vice president when he was 47 but lost.
- He ran for Senate when he was 49 but lost.
- He was finally elected president of the United States at age 51.
- He changed history, especially for African-American citizens, when he was 53.

 Of course, the answer is Abraham Lincoln. Whenever you think about your failures, think about Abraham Lincoln. He overcame many failures and became a successful president, contributing so much to our country.

Stress Buster Five: Don't Imagine Being Scared!

Everyone has an imagination. In fact, imaginations make life very exciting. Without your imagination, you would never be able to let yourself believe that the monsters in the movies are real, or, when you look at the stars, you would not have any fun wondering if someone else was living on another planet in the universe. Your imagination can make life fun, interesting, and even pleasant if you use it in the right way. Sometimes, however, we do not use our imaginations in ways that are helpful. This is especially true with fear. When children (or adults) fear a situation or a challenge, it is usually because their fantasies and their imaginations get out of hand. Instead of thinking, "I have a test tomorrow," a student may think, "I have a test tomorrow that is going to be harder than a million tests put together. When I fail it, I will be the most stupid person in the world!" None of this is true. It is unlikely that any test can be as hard as a million tests put together, and doing poorly on a test does not mean you are stupid.

When you have a fear, whether it is about a test or another challenge, think about it before you let yourself get stressed. How much of your fear is in your imagination? How real does your fear seem to you? How much of your fear IS real? You will be surprised to learn that, if you really think about your fears and worries, many of them feel much worse than they actually are.

Stress Buster Six: What Does Test Anxiety Feel Like?

It is important to know what it feels like to be anxious or stressed. "Anxiety" is a word that describes your feelings when you worry or are afraid. When you know how it feels, you can ask for help. You can also see if those terrible feelings are worth all the trouble they cause by asking yourself, "Did things turn out as badly as I thought?" Most of the time, everything turns out just fine.

Every student who has test anxiety knows it is not a good feeling! Work through these exercises to think about how it feels to be anxious.

Below, make a list of "feeling" words that describe how it feels to be scared.

_____

_____

Now, write down times when you had these feelings and how things turned out in the end. Did what you were scared of really happen? Did anything really bad happen to you? Will you be scared during this experience again? What did you learn from the experience?

_____

_____

Stress Buster Seven: How We Learn—Three Ways!

1. **Doing something over and over again.**
   How did you learn to read? You might have said your ABCs hundreds of times and read simple "baby books" over and over. Slowly, you learned how to read. You learn about yourself in the same way. If your parents tell you over and over that you are smart or kind, you come to believe it. If school is always hard, day after day, you start to feel that you aren't very smart. You may be smart, but you don't believe it. Though it seems as though you can't do well in school, it may not be true.

2. **Having something REALLY BIG happen.**

   If you eat a hot pepper in one bite, you will never forget it! No one will ever have to say to you again, "Don't eat that hot pepper!" You have already learned your lesson. Sometimes, one scary experience is enough to teach you a lesson once and for all.

   While it may be helpful to learn not to eat a hot pepper in one bite, sometimes you learn things that are not helpful. Suppose you had to recite a poem in front of your class and you made an embarrassing mistake. Instead of saying, "The rain was coming down so hard," you said, "The 'lane' was coming down so hard." Everyone laughed and teased you. This experience made you believe that it is terrible to get up in front of your class. Making the mistake in front of your class probably hurt, much like eating a hot pepper would. You learned that you didn't want to go through either experience ever again. But it is not helpful to think this about the class experience. Even though you made a mistake once, that does not mean you will have the same experience each time. A hot pepper is always hot, but you can control experiences like talking in front of your class.

3. **Generalization.**
   This fairly big word means you take something you learned in one place or situation and use it in other places or situations.

   Let's take the hot pepper problem. You learn that hot peppers burn. You use this information to think twice before eating anything that looks like a hot pepper. Generalization, however, can go too far. You might get worried about eating anything green, such as a green grape or a green bean. Soon, you might not try any foods that look "weird" or "spicy." Your fear of new foods seems pretty real, even though most new foods aren't really as hot as the pepper. The same is true for tests. Don't let one hard test scare you away from all tests!

© 2004 Englefield & Associates, Inc.

Stress Buster Eight: What Kind of Thoughts Seem "Real" To You?

Kids have different thoughts and ideas that lead to test anxiety and stress. You learn these ideas in a lot of ways. Which kid describes how you feel?

Stay-Away Stephanie
Stephanie's thoughts tell her that it is better to stay away from challenges, especially tests. Stephanie believes that anything is better than having to take tests. She tries to fool herself into thinking that nothing could be worse than taking a test. Stephanie tries to forget about the problems that will happen if she stays away. "If I stay home sick, I won't have to take the test. I don't care if I get a detention; I'm not taking the test." Stay-Away Stephanie feels less nervous when she doesn't face a test, but she never learns to face her fears.

Worried Wendy
Wendy always thinks the worst will happen. Her mind is like a disaster movie, and her thoughts just make her more and more anxious. "What if I can't answer all the questions? What if I don't do well? My teacher will not like me. I'll lose all my friends." Wendy is always watching and waiting for the worst thing to happen. She spends her time worrying instead of figuring out how to do well.

Critical Chris
Chris spends all his time putting himself down. No matter what, he always sees himself as not able to do much. When he gets a B+, he says to himself, "I made a lot of stupid mistakes, so I didn't get an A." He never compliments himself, "I did AWESOME getting a B+." He feels bad about himself all of the time and never notices what he does well. Chris can't appreciate it when he does well. As a result, he feels he will fail at whatever he tries.

Victim Vince
Vince can't take responsibility for himself. He thinks everything is controlled by others and that he can't control his life. "They'll make that test too hard for me; all the teachers are against me." "If my weird little brother didn't make so much noise, I could study better." Vince thinks that nothing he does will help; the world is against him. He often feels hopeless, sad, and worried.

Perfect Pat
Pat studies and studies. She has one favorite word: <u>should</u>. "I <u>should</u> study more. I <u>should</u> write this book report over." Trying hard is fine, but Pat works so much that she never feels like she has done enough. She also worries because she feels there is more to know. Pat needs to spend more time learning how to study and find time to relax.

Stress Buster Nine: Changing Negative Ideas into Positive Ideas

You have to convince yourself that some of your ideas may not be correct or helpful even though they seem very real. Ask yourself questions to see if these ideas are true. Read these questions and fill in the blanks about a negative thought you have about tests or other difficult situations. Play detective!

What is a negative thought I have about tests?

_____

What evidence is there that my idea is true?

_____

What evidence is there that my idea isn't true?

_____

If I believe my negative ideas, what will happen?

_____

If I believe ideas that are more positive, what will happen?

_____

Stress Buster Ten: How to Create Positive Ideas

Positive ideas are strong ideas. No one ever does anything important by having "weak" ideas. What would have happened if Christopher Columbus had said, "Well, I guess I can make it out there exploring the world, but it might not work out. Maybe I'll get seasick. I'll miss my mom. I wish I had studied more in Sailor School!" He probably never would have been a successful explorer!

Making a positive statement has three parts.
1. Use the word "**I**." "**I** am as smart as anyone else. **I** can do well on this test."
2. Avoid using the word "not." Say to yourself, "I will be calm during the test," instead of "I will not be nervous during the test."
3. Think the opposite of your negative idea. If math is your poor subject, state, "I can think clearly about a lot of things, so I can give math a good shot."

Stress Buster Eleven: How to Face the Test Monster

There are other ways to overcome test anxiety, and some of them are even fun to do!

1. Draw a picture of how a person looks when he or she succeeds on a test. Drawing lets you imagine how you can tackle a problem. You might want to draw cartoon figures or even animals instead of people. You might want to draw yourself!

2. Give yourself 10 points for every thought or idea that helps you think positively about yourself and about tests. Write them down. Ask your parents if they can post your list on the refrigerator when you reach 100 points.

Thought	Number of Times I Thought This	Points

3. Pay attention to all the good things about yourself. Feeling good about yourself will generalize into feeling good about taking tests and doing other things in your life. Make a list of good things to say about yourself, especially in school.

_____

_____

_____

Test-Taking Strategies

Test-Taking Strategies: Skills You Can Use throughout Life

A **test-taking strategy** is a skill that you learn to help you do well on tests. Strategies help you perform to the best of your ability, especially on the Ohio Achievement Test (OAT) for Grade 4. Once you have learned and practiced these special skills, you will feel more confident in yourself because you know something about taking tests that you didn't know before. You will be "test smart." You will have taken the time to prepare for the test; you will have practiced taking the test; and you will have learned the best strategies for succeeding on the test.

In this chapter, you will review the three different kinds of questions you will see on the OAT for Grade 4: multiple-choice, short-answer, and extended-response questions. You will learn special strategies for answering test questions in Reading and Mathematics. You will also learn strategies to help you do well on the Writing section.

Strategies for Success

1. Luck Isn't Enough!

Have you ever had a lucky number, a lucky color, or even a lucky hat? Everyone believes in luck; some do more than others. A famous NFL quarterback never wears new shoes if he has won a game while wearing one particular pair. It probably doesn't make sense (new shoes might be better for gripping the turf and staying on his feet), but he thinks it helps. If he just believed in luck, however, he wouldn't be a successful NFL player. He also has to learn plays and practice daily! Learning in your classroom and practicing what you learn are some of the best strategies you can have. Don't be like Chuck!

There was a cool boy named Chuck,
Who thought taking tests was just luck.
He never prepared.
He said, "I'm not scared."
When his test scores appear, he should duck!

2. Don't Rush. Speeding through the Test Doesn't Help.

Speeding through the test doesn't help. In our world, speed seems important. You often hear about the fastest computer, the fastest running back, and the world's fastest bullet train. Speed does get people's attention in some situations, but how fast you complete the OAT for Grade 4 does not make your test score better. It is important to show what you know, not how fast you can answer questions.

There was a fourth grader named Liz,
Who sped through her test like a whiz.
She thought she should race
At a very fast pace,
But it caused her to mess up her quiz.

3. **Read Directions Carefully!**
Sometimes, you might make up your mind about things before you explore and study them. Other times, you may feel nervous or rushed and forget to read or listen carefully. You may have problems with tests if you do not read and remember directions. You may think you already know what you will be asked, and you rush through the directions. This does not help you do your best!

Imagine you are a famous chef. You are really well known for your cakes. You make the best cakes in Ohio! One day, a group of visiting kings and queens comes to Ohio for a very important visit. You are asked to bake a special cake for them, one you have never baked before. You are given a list of ingredients and directions, but you barely look at them. You think to yourself, "Who has time? And, anyway, I know how to bake any cake without much direction." Unfortunately, you don't read that the cake needs to bake at 250 degrees for 15 minutes. You have always baked your cakes at 350 degrees for 30 minutes. What do you get? Crispy cake and upset royalty–not a good combination!

Reading directions slowly, repeating them to yourself, asking yourself if the directions make sense, and calming yourself down are powerful test-taking strategies. Think about Fred.

There was a nice boy named Fred,
Who ignored almost all that he read.
The directions were easy,
But he said, "I don't need these!"
He should have read them instead.

4. **Don't Get Stuck on One Question.**
Generally, everyone wants to do a good job. Few people want to give up when faced with a question that is difficult. Some people panic or get really nervous when they come across a question they can't seem to answer. Letting yourself get stuck on a difficult question is a poor strategy for two reasons. One, on the OAT for Grade 4, incorrectly answering one question is not a big problem. The test has lots of questions, and you are given plenty of opportunities to show what you know. Two, scientists who have studied learning and remembering have found that, when students go on to other questions, it may actually help them figure out answers later. Think about Von!

There was a sweet girl named Von,
Who got stuck and just couldn't go on.
She'd sit there and stare,
But the answer wasn't there.
Before she knew it, all the time was gone.

5. Power Guessing Can Help!

Let's say your brother takes your special key chain. He takes it off your dresser right in front of your eyes! Then, he puts his hands behind his back and says, "It's in one of my fists."

You can't see where he has put it. You ask him to show you his fists. He says, "You have to guess which hand the key chain is in." How do you make the best possible guess? Well, you look for clues! Use the knowledge and tools you have; you have more than you think. Look at his hands. Is one hand closed tighter than the other? Is your brother right- or left-handed? Does he use one hand more often than the other? Do his eyes look at one hand in particular?

If you use these clues, you are "power guessing." Your chances of succeeding are greater because you are using what you already know to guess. You might not know the exact answer, but you have some ideas that may help. Your teacher will have many ideas about power guessing on the OAT.

Power guessing is a helpful strategy. There is no penalty for guessing. You might have learned that guessing is bad and thinking is good. Actually, guessing and thinking can go together with great results! It's OK to guess, and guessing is even better when you learn how to power guess. Think about Tess!

There was a smart girl named Tess,
Who thought it was useless to guess.
If a question was tough,
She just gave up,
Which only added to her stress.

6. What Happens if I Don't Do Well on the Test?

Assessment tests are a way to measure what you have learned up to the fourth grade. Keep in mind that it is important to do your best on tests, but receiving a low score does not mean that your friends, parents, or teachers won't like you. Think about Chad.

There was a nice boy named Chad,
Who thought if he failed he was bad.
His teacher said, "That's not true.
I like you no matter how you do."
Now Chad is glad and not sad.

7. **Don't Be Too Calm or Too Scared.**
Think about cavemen and saber-toothed tigers. There was a time when humans had to cope with large and scary animals all of the time. Humans who tried to forget about the dangers of big animals usually found themselves in life-threatening situations. Humans who became easily terrified usually ran the wrong way in the woods and became lost or were eaten by those unfriendly animals. The people who did the best were the ones who recognized the danger, became a little bit concerned about what would happen, and planned how they would escape and take care of themselves.

Taking tests seriously is important. You cannot ignore tests or let tests take over all of your thinking. Here's what happened to two sisters.

There was a student named Claire,
Who usually said, "I don't care."
Her sister named Bess,
Always felt total stress.
They weren't a successful pair!

8. **Be as Neat as Possible.**
No student is perfectly neat, but being as neat as possible will help you on the test. It will be hard for others to read your good ideas if they can't read your writing. During the test, you have to print or write clearly. Unreadable or out-of-place answers on the test cannot be graded. Try to do your best! Think about Rob.

There was good guy named Rob,
Who was cute but really a slob!
You couldn't read his writing,
Because it was frightening!
When his test score comes, he will sob!

9. **Don't Be Afraid to Mark in Your Test Booklet.**
The test booklets are created with a large amount of empty space surrounding the test questions so that you can write down ideas or figure out math problems in margins and boxes. There is no penalty for writing in the blank areas of your test booklet.

> There was a kid named Dirk
> Who didn't show his work.
> He could write on the side.
> His paper was WIDE!
> But he didn't think and look.

General Test-Taking Strategies for Multiple-Choice Questions

All multiple-choice questions on the OAT for Grade 4 have four possible answer choices, only one of which is correct. There is no penalty for "power guessing." Choices such as "Not Here" and "Make no change" will appear on the test; when you see these choices, be sure you know they mean "the answer is not provided" and "the text is correct." The Writing, Reading, and Mathematics tests include multiple-choice questions. The following strategies will help you with multiple-choice questions.

- **Use Your Pencil.**
  A pencil isn't just for writing answers. Using your pencil can help you in several different ways. You can use your pencil to cross out choices that are wrong. Pencils can also be used to make notes in your test booklet. This can help you remember ideas or figure out problems. You can make notes of ideas to help you answer questions or to work out math problems. You can also use your pencil to underline or circle important "key words" in questions. These "key words" help you find the correct answer.

  If you are stuck on a question, use your pencil to circle the test question number, then move on. You can return to those questions later on during the testing period. Use the following question to practice the pencil strategy.

  Where would you find how many people lived in Cleveland in 1960?
  ○ A. an almanac
  ○ B. a thesaurus
  ○ C. a dictionary
  ○ D. an atlas

You should have marked the words, "Where" and "how many people," in the question. These words tell you what is important in the question. Choice D is incorrect because an atlas is a book of maps. Choice C should be crossed out because the dictionary gives definitions and meanings of words, not population information. Choice B should be crossed out because the thesaurus is a reference book containing word synonyms; it does not give information on the number of people living in cities. Therefore, Choice A is correct. Don't forget to use your pencil. It is a powerful tool!

- **Filling in the Answer Bubble Is Important!**
  You must learn to use a No. 2 pencil and fill in answer bubbles correctly.

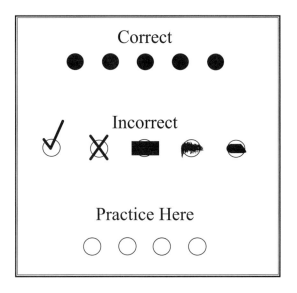

- **Read the Question and ALL the Answer Choices Carefully.**
  Remember Fred, who never read the directions? Well, don't be like him! Instead, use your eyes, take a deep breath, and start at the top of the page or the beginning of the question. Pay attention to questions AND answer choices. Search for "key words" in the questions AND the answers. Look at this example.

    If Chad has 2 dogs and 3 goldfish, what is the total number of pets he has?
    ○ A. 2 pets
    ○ B. 3 pets
    ○ C. 5 pets
    ○ D. 6 pets

Look at the answers. Mark important words in the question. You should have marked "2 dogs and 3 goldfish" and "total number of pets." Right away, the word "total" should tell you to add. Choices A and B should be crossed out because they are numbers taken from the question without using addition. Two answer choices are now left to choose from. After adding 2 and 3, you should get 5. Choice C is the correct answer.

- **Don't Always Go with Your First Answer.**
  Sometimes, more than one answer may seem right. Slow down and read all the answer choices. Ask yourself, "What does each answer choice mean?" Look at this example:

  What is the opposite of the word <u>light</u>?

  ○ A. black

  ○ B. lamp

  ○ C. night

  ○ D. dark

  At first, all the answer choices may look correct. Choice B is incorrect because it is something that provides light. Choices A and C are both answers that remind you of what the correct answer actually is but are not really the opposite of the word "light." The correct answer is Choice D, "dark."

- **Use Your Common Sense.**
  Common sense means using information you already know to answer difficult questions. When taking a test, look at the question and think about each answer choice. Your common sense will help you see information that is familiar to you. This information may help you pick the correct answer. Consider the following question.

  John went to the store to buy an apple to <u>consume</u>. What does the word <u>consume</u> mean?

  ○ A. went

  ○ B. buy

  ○ C. apple

  ○ D. eat

  At first, all the answer choices may look correct. Choice C can be eliminated because it is a noun, not a verb. Although Choices A and B are both words that are found in the sentence, neither makes sense if substituted for the word "consume" in the sentence. Choice D, the correct answer, should make sense because an apple is something you eat.

- **Use Partial Knowledge.**
  You know more than you think. You have learned all kinds of information from reading, watching TV, talking to your family and friends, and traveling. Using partial knowledge is using the information you have gained throughout your life to help you answer test questions. Consider this example.

  Which unit of measure should be used to measure the distance from Columbus to Cleveland?
  - ○ A. centimeters
  - ○ B. liters
  - ○ C. kilometers
  - ○ D. ounces

  Use partial knowledge to find incorrect answers. Choice A can be crossed out because you know from using a ruler that centimeters measure small lengths. You have also seen liters of soda or juice at the grocery store. You know that liters measure liquids, not distance. Ounces measure small weights. Therefore, Choices B and D are wrong. This leaves the correct choice, "kilometers," which is Choice C.

You will also have to answer short-answer and extended-response questions. These are questions for which you have to fill in the answer. Some questions will only require one or two words or short phrases, but other questions may require a full sentence or two. Remember to write clearly and neatly so that people can read what you have written. Correct spelling and proper grammar will help make your response clear. However, if you misspell a word or forget to use a comma or period, it will not be counted against you. The most important thing to remember when you answer short-answer and extended-response questions is to completely answer the question as best you can.

General Test-Taking Strategies for a Great Writing Composition

The Grade 4 Writing test will also include two writing prompts that you will need to write a response to. Use the following strategies to help you do well on your writing composition.

1. Carefully read each prompt.
2. Make notes and organize your thoughts in the margins of the test booklet.
3. Skim the prompt again to help you think of more ideas for your answer.
4. Use the information box provided to help you write each composition. It will remind you how to write a good composition.
5. Write each response in several paragraphs using sentences. Make sure you give some details and explain your thoughts clearly.
6. Read the prompt again to check that you have addressed all parts of the prompt.

Test-Taking Strategies for Specific Areas

Reading Test
There are multiple-choice, short-answer, and extended-response questions on the Reading test. Here are some good strategies to use on the Reading test.

- **Read the Question Carefully.**
  It may help to look over the questions before and after you read through the passage. As you read the passage, look for information that may help you answer the questions.

- **Look for Key Words.**
  Remember, you can write in your test booklet. As you read through the different passages, circle or underline important words you come across. Make notes in the margin with ideas that seem to answer the question.

- **Review What You Read to Find More Details.**
  If you don't think you can answer the question, reread the passage and look for more details.

- **Ask Yourself, "Did I Answer the Question?"**
  Read the answer choice you think is correct or the response you have written to make sure you have answered the question correctly.

- **Circle the Numbers of the Questions You Cannot Answer.**
  If you are not sure of the correct answer, circle the question number and return to it later in the test.

- **Do Not Immediately Pick Your First Answer.**
  Your first choice could be the correct choice, but it could also be a wrong answer that a test maker used to distract you. Recheck your answers.

Writing Test
The Writing test is different from the other subjects on the OAT for Grade 4. Along with multiple-choice questions, you will be asked to write two compositions based on writing prompts. You can use the style of writing you feel most comfortable with, but you cannot choose poetry.

- **Think about Ideas Freely, but Stay "on Topic."**
  Write down ideas that make sense and tell the reader about the subject. Don't write about other things. For example, if you are asked to write about an airplane trip, you might write about planes you have seen, a plane trip you have taken, or how you imagine it might feel in an airplane. Don't include ideas that aren't about airplanes, such as a bicycle trip or a day at the pool. These ideas are about trips or vacations, not about airplane rides!

- **Use Your Pencil.**
  Write down ideas, circle or underline key words, and practice spelling.

- **Self-Edit.**
Review your finished work to check for errors in spelling, punctuation, capitalization, and completeness of sentences and ideas.

- **Use a Checklist.**
A writing checklist will be given to you in this book and on the OAT for Grade 4. You should use it to complete your writing composition. The checklist contains many ideas you need to think about as you are writing. When you complete your writing sample, make sure you have used most of the important reminders from the checklist.

Mathematics Test
The Mathematics section of the OAT for Grade 4 will ask you to answer multiple-choice, short-answer, and extended-response questions.

- **Rechecking Your Work is Important.**
Always recheck your answers to math problems. Rechecking problems may be very helpful if you have time left at the end of the test.

- **You Can Draw a Table, Chart, or Picture to Help You Answer the Question.**
Diagramming or drawing what you already know can help you find the right answer. Consider this example.

Marcus raids his grandmother's freezer with his three friends, looking for a late-night dessert snack. His grandmother has several types of ice cream and cookies in her freezer, but not very much of each one. In fact, for each flavor of ice cream, she only has enough for one serving, and she only has one cookie of each kind. His grandmother has five different types of ice cream: chocolate chip, fudge ripple, strawberry, vanilla, and orange. His grandmother also has five different cookies: chocolate chip, sugar, peanut butter, raisin, and oatmeal. Because Marcus is a polite young man, he lets his three friends choose their favorite ice cream and favorite cookie first.

Dessert Diagram
Marcus' choices after his friends choose their snacks:

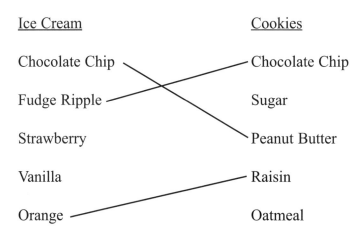

After his friends have made their choices, how many types of ice cream and cookies are left for Marcus to choose from?

- ○ A. 2 types of ice cream and 1 type of cookie
- ○ B. 2 types of ice cream and 2 types of cookies
- ○ C. 1 type of ice cream and 2 types of cookies
- ○ D. 3 types of ice cream and 3 types of cookies

Using the diagram, you can see there are 2 types of ice cream and 2 types of cookies left for Marcus to choose from.

If Marcus can pick one type of ice cream and one type of cookie to go together, how many combinations are available after his friends have chosen their snacks?

- ○ A. 2 combinations
- ○ B. 3 combinations
- ○ C. 4 combinations
- ○ D. 8 combinations

Again, use the diagram to help you. Marcus has four combinations to choose from. He can pick strawberry ice cream and a sugar cookie; strawberry ice cream and an oatmeal cookie; vanilla ice cream and a sugar cookie; or vanilla ice cream and an oatmeal cookie.

Writing

Introduction

In the Writing section of the Ohio Achievement Test (OAT), you will be asked questions to test what you have learned so far in school. These questions are based on the writing skills you have been taught in school through fourth grade. The questions you will answer are not meant to confuse or trick you but are written so you have the best chance to show what you know.

Questions I Will Answer on the OAT

The Writing OAT has two sections. In the first section, you will be given two writing prompts. Respond to each prompt using any type of writing you choose, except poetry. You have many types of writing to choose from, such as a narrative (a story), a journal entry, an essay, a letter, etc., but you may not use poetry to write your composition. As you respond to each prompt, use the graphic organizer, the Revising Checklist, and the Editing Checklist to help you write your composition.

In the second section of the Writing OAT, you will answer 15 questions about spelling, punctuation and capitalization, and grammar and usage. Look at the underlined words and determine if they are correct or not. If they are incorrect, either write the correct answer on the line or fill in the circle next to the correct answer.

The Kitchen

My <u>favarite</u> room in the house is the kitchen. I love to eat, so that's my number one reason. There are other reasons, too. I love the yummy smells that come from <u>The Oven</u> when a cake or cookies are baking. I love the way the kitchen sounds: bacon sizzling in a frying pan or the kettle whistling on the stove.

1. My <u>favarite</u> room in the house is the kitchen.

    favorite
    _____

    ☐ The word is spelled correctly as is.

2. I love the yummy smells that come from <u>The Oven</u> when a cake or cookies are baking.

    ○ A. the Oven
    ○ B. The oven
    ● C. the oven
    ○ D. Correct as is

Item Distribution on the OAT for Grade 4 Writing

	Multiple Choice (1 point)	Writing Prompts (16 points each)	Points
	15	—	15
	—	1 Informational Report OR Response to Literature	16
	—	1 Narrative Account OR Formal/Informal Letter	16
Number of Scored Items	15	2	—
Total Numbers		17 items	47 points

Note: This is the Item Distribution that will be used on the actual OAT for Grade 4 Writing. Each practice test in this book has 20 multiple-choice questions and two writing prompts. Due to space constraints, there are only two pages of writing lines in this book for each writing prompt. On the actual OAT, there will be four pages of writing lines.

Scoring

On the OAT for Grade 4 Writing, you will be tested with 15 multiple-choice writing conventions items worth 1 point each, and two writing prompts worth up to 16 points each. The total number of points from the multiple-choice test items and the two writing prompts will determine your Writing test score.

Rubrics

The OAT for Grade 4 Writing consists of two writing prompts. Each writing prompt will be scored using a 4-point holistic rubric. Two test readers will read and score each prompt. Each writing prompt is worth up to 16 points. Below is a sample of a 4-point rubric a reader would use to score your prompt:

A **4-point** response focuses on the topic, clearly addresses the purpose (mode), and has ample supporting details. It has a logical structure that flows naturally with a beginning, a middle, and an end. It has a sense of wholeness. It has an effective use of language with a variety of words and sentence patterns. It shows an awareness of word usage and spelling patterns in commonly used words. It exhibits the use of capital letters at the beginning of sentences and for proper nouns. It contains correct end punctuation.

A **3-point** response is related to the topic and generally addresses the purpose (mode). It has adequate supporting details. It has a logical order with an apparent beginning, middle, and end, although some lapses may occur. It has word choice that are generally adequate and has sentences that are mostly complete. It shows an awareness of word usage and spelling patterns in commonly used words. It may have occasional word usage, spelling errors, and punctuation errors that do not interfere with the message. It has correct capitalization (at the beginning of sentences and for proper nouns).

A **2-point** response attempts to address the purpose (mode). It demonstrates an awareness of the topic but may include extraneous or loosely related material. It includes some supporting details. It shows an attempt at organizing the paper around a beginning, middle, and end. It has limited vocabulary and has word usage and spelling errors that interfere with the message. It shows knowledge of capitalization at the beginning of sentences and for proper nouns. It shows knowledge of the conventions of punctuation.

A **1-point** response may or may not attempt to address the purpose (mode). It offers few details and is only slightly related to the topic. It exhibits little or no evidence of an organizational structure; the beginning, middle, or end of the response may be poorly defined or nonexistent. It has limited or inappropriate vocabulary that obscures meaning. It has gross errors in sentence structure, word usage, and spelling that impede communication. It has frequent and blatant errors in basic punctuation and in capitalization at the beginning of sentences and for proper nouns.

A **Zero** is assigned if there is no response or if the response indicates no understanding of the concept or activity.

A **NS (Not Scorable)** is assigned if the response is unreadable, illegible, or written in a language other than English.

Directions for Practice Test 1

This Grade 4 Writing Achievement Practice Test has 20 questions. These questions will test you on how well you understand and apply punctuation, grammar, and spelling. You will also be given two writing prompts to use to complete two compositions.

There are several important things to remember as you take this test:
- Read each question carefully. Think about what is being asked. Then write your answer on the blank line, check the box, or fill in one answer bubble to mark your answer, depending on the type of question.
- If you do not know the answer to a multiple-choice question, skip it and go on. If you have time, go back to the questions you skipped and answer them.
- For the writing prompts, write your response on the lines provided.
- Use the Revising and Editing checklists to help with your compositions.
- If you finish the Practice Test early, go back and check over your work.

Write an informational report about fireflies. Use the information in the graphic organizer to write your report. Use the facts and details you have been given. Make sure your report has an introduction, a body, and a conclusion. Remember to use the Revising Checklist and the Editing Checklist at the end of the writing activity to check your work.

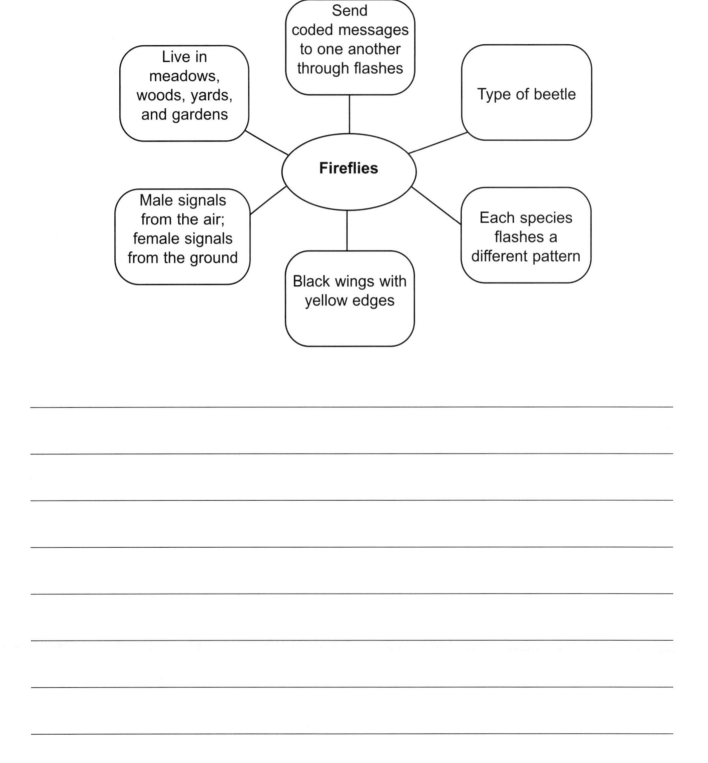

Revising Checklist

☐ I used facts and details from the graphic organizer in my report.

☐ My report gives information about fireflies.

☐ My report has an introduction, a body, and a conclusion.

☐ I re-read my report and it makes sense.

Editing Checklist

☐ I double-checked my spelling.

☐ I double-checked my punctuation.

☐ I double-checked my capitalization.

☐ I double-checked to make sure all of my sentences are complete.

Think of a time when something funny happened to you or you saw something funny. Write a <u>narrative</u> (story) telling about what happened. Be sure to include <u>in detail</u>:
- The place (setting)
- The people who were there (characters)
- The events (plot)

Remember to use the Revising Checklist and the Editing Checklist at the end of the writing activity to check your work.

Story Title:

Where does the story take place? (Setting)	Who is in the story? (Characters)
_____	_____
	_____

What happens in the story? (Plot)

Events:
1. _____
2. _____
3. _____
Ending: _____
_____

_____

_____

_____

_____

_____

_____

Go to next page ➡

Revising Checklist

☐ I used facts and details from the graphic organizer in my story.

☐ My story is about something funny that happened to me or that I saw.

☐ My story has an introduction, a body, and a conclusion.

☐ I re-read my story and it makes sense.

Editing Checklist

☐ I double-checked my spelling.

☐ I double-checked my punctuation.

☐ I double-checked my capitalization.

☐ I double-checked to make sure all of my sentences are complete.

Go to next page

Directions: Spelling Activities—Use the selection to answer Questions 1–7. If the underlined word is not spelled correctly, write the correct spelling of the word on the line provided. If the underlined word is spelled correctly, mark the box with an X.

Missing Luck

I looked everywere for my missing sock. It wasn't an everyday sock; it was one half of my pair of lucky sockes. These socks helped me score a goal during every soccer match. These socks made me run fast. With my lucky socks I could turn on a dime and move efforrtlessly. Now, half of my luck was gone. I found one lucky sock on top of the drier, and I put it on. I grabbed a no-luck sock from the laundry basket and went to look for my shues. "Some luck is better than no luck," I thought.

1. I looked everywere for my missing sock.

   _____

   ☐ The word is spelled correctly as is.

2. It wasn't an everyday sock; it was one half of my pair of lucky sockes.

   _____

   ☐ The word is spelled correctly as is.

3. These socks helped me score a goal during every soccer match.

   _____

   ☐ The word is spelled correctly as is.

4. With my lucky socks I could turn on a dime and move efforrtlessly.

_____

☐ The word is spelled correctly as is.

5. I found one lucky sock on top of the drier, and I put it on.

_____

☐ The word is spelled correctly as is.

6. I grabbed a no-luck sock from the laundry basket and went to look for my shues.

_____

☐ The word is spelled correctly as is.

7. "Some luck is better than no luck," I thought.

_____

☐ The word is spelled correctly as is.

Directions: Punctuation and Capitalization Activities—Use the selection to answer Questions 8–13. If what is <u>underlined</u> is not correct, either fill in the circle next to the correct answer or write it correctly on the line provided.

Two Wheels

Even though Kaya was in the fourth <u>grade she</u> had never ridden a bike without training wheels. There weren't many kids in the neighborhood, so <u>Kaya</u> only took bike rides with her parents. Kids might have made fun of her four wheels, but her parents never did. They sometimes suggested removing the extra <u>wheels Kaya</u> always said, "No. There's no reason to ride on two wheels when four are OK for <u>me.</u> She grew used to the extra support, and she was afraid of losing <u>it?</u> "Maybe one day I'll take the training wheels <u>off,</u> she thought, "but not today."

8. Even though Kaya was in the fourth <u>grade she</u> had never ridden a bike without training wheels.

   ○ A. grade. She
   ○ B. grade; she
   ○ C. grade, she
   ○ D. Correct as is

9. There weren't many kids in the neighborhood, so <u>Kaya</u> only took bike rides with her parents.

   ☐ The word uses correct capitalization as is.

10. They sometimes suggested removing the extra <u>wheels Kaya</u> always said, "No.

    ○ A. wheels. Kaya
    ○ B. wheels? Kaya
    ○ C. wheels! Kaya
    ○ D. Correct as is

11. "No. There's no reason to ride on two wheels when four are OK for me.

    ○ A. for me!
    ○ B. for me."
    ○ C. for me?"
    ○ D. Correct as is

12. She grew used to the extra support, and she was afraid of losing it?

    ○ A. it.
    ○ B. it;
    ○ C. it,
    ○ D. Correct as is

13. "Maybe one day I'll take the training wheels off, she thought, "but not today."

    ○ A. off.
    ○ B. off,"
    ○ C. off;"
    ○ D. Correct as is

Directions: Grammar and Usage Activities—Use the selection to answer Questions 14–20. If the underlined word is not correct, fill in the circle next to the correct answer.

The Legend of Happy and Sad

The town of Silly Place was in a valley between the very large and very wide Granger Mountains. The people who <u>lives</u> in Silly Place were filled with laughter. They laughed when they were happy or sad, during good times or bad times, if they were joyful or upset. No matter what the reason, the people of Silly Place <u>laughs</u>.

One day, a stranger wandered into Silly Place because his sheep <u>taken</u> him on a journey across the mountains. No one had ever wandered into Silly Place, <u>and</u> the frightened townspeople began to laugh. The stranger was also frightened, but instead of laughing, he cried. The people of Silly Place didn't understand why he <u>was</u> crying, and the stranger explained that he only knew how to cry. In his town, everyone cried when they were happy or sad; they did not know any other way. Since no one knew if laughing meant you were happy or sad, the people of Silly Place decided to laugh when they were happy and cry when <u>its</u> were sad. The stranger <u>tolds</u> his story to the people of his town when he returned. People have both laughed and cried ever since.

14. The people who <u>lives</u> in Silly Place were filled with laughter.

    ○ A. lived
    ○ B. living
    ○ C. live
    ○ D. Correct as is

15. No matter what the reason, the people of Silly Place <u>laughs</u>.

    ○ A. laugh
    ○ B. laughed
    ○ C. laughen
    ○ D. Correct as is

16. One day, a stranger wandered into Silly Place because his sheep taken him on a journey across the mountains.

    ○ A. take
    ○ B. taked
    ○ C. took
    ○ D. Correct as is

17. No one had ever wandered into Silly Place, and the frightened townspeople began to laugh.

    ○ A. but
    ○ B. since
    ○ C. because
    ○ D. Correct as is

18. The people of Silly Place didn't understand why he was crying, and the stranger explained that he only knew how to cry.

    ○ A. were
    ○ B. did
    ○ C. is
    ○ D. Correct as is

19. Since no one knew if laughing meant you were happy or sad, the people of Silly Place decided to laugh when they were happy and cry when its were sad.

    ○ A. it
    ○ B. they
    ○ C. them
    ○ D. Correct as is

20. The stranger tolds his story to the people of his town when he returned.

    ○ A. told
    ○ B. tell
    ○ C. tells
    ○ D. Correct as is

Directions for Practice Test 2

This Grade 4 Writing Achievement Practice Test has 20 questions. These questions will test you on how well you understand and apply punctuation, grammar, and spelling. You will also be given two writing prompts to use to complete two compositions.

There are several important things to remember as you take this test:
- Read each question carefully. Think about what is being asked. Then write your answer on the blank line, check the box, or fill in one answer bubble to mark your answer, depending on the type of question.
- If you do not know the answer to a multiple-choice question, skip it and go on. If you have time, go back to the questions you skipped and answer them.
- For the writing prompts, write your response on the lines provided.
- Use the Revising and Editing checklists to help with your compositions.
- If you finish the Practice Test early, go back and check over your work.

Think about the most memorable school assembly you have ever attended. Write a <u>narrative</u> (story) telling about what happened at the assembly. Be sure to include <u>in detail</u>:
- The place (setting)
- The people who were there (characters)
- The events (plot)

Remember to use the Revising Checklist and the Editing Checklist at the end of the writing activity to check your work.

Story Title:

Where does the story take place? (Setting)	Who is in the story? (Characters)

What happens in the story? (Plot)

Events:
1. _____
2. _____
3. _____

Ending: _____

Revising Checklist

☐ I used facts and details from the graphic organizer in my story.

☐ My story is about the most memorable school assembly I've ever attended.

☐ My story has an introduction, a body, and a conclusion.

☐ I re-read my story and it makes sense.

Editing Checklist

☐ I double-checked my spelling.

☐ I double-checked my punctuation.

☐ I double-checked my capitalization.

☐ I double-checked to make sure all of my sentences are complete.

Go to next page

Write an <u>essay</u> telling about how you and your best friend are alike and how you are different. Be sure to include <u>in detail</u>:
- Who you are writing about
- How you are similar
- How you are different

Remember to use the Revising Checklist and the Editing Checklist at the end of the writing activity to check your work.

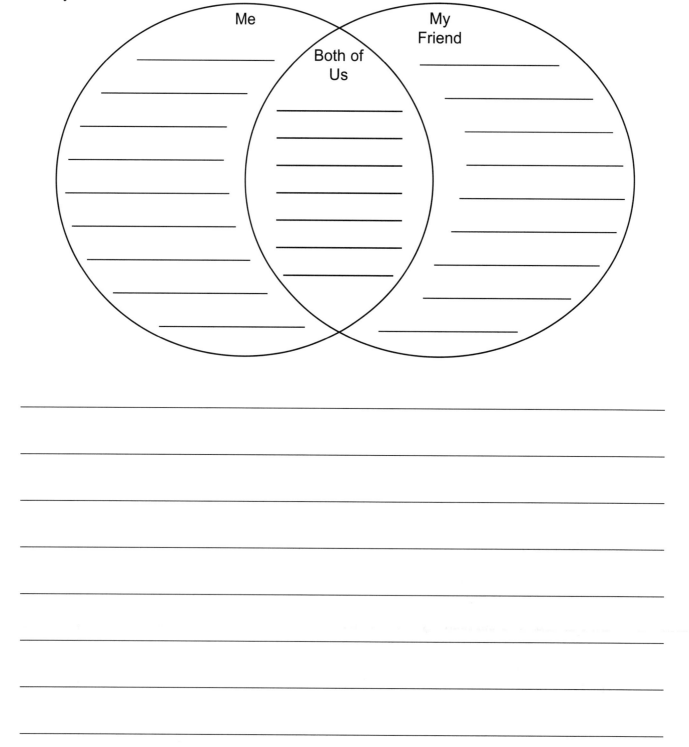

Revising Checklist

☐ I wrote about my best friend and me.

☐ I wrote in detail about how we are the same.

☐ I wrote in detail about how we are different.

☐ I re-read my essay and it makes sense.

Editing Checklist

☐ I double-checked my spelling.

☐ I double-checked my punctuation.

☐ I double-checked my capitalization.

☐ I double-checked to make sure all of my sentences are complete.

Directions: Spelling Activities—Use the selection to answer Questions 1–6. If the underlined word is not spelled correctly, write the correct spelling of the word on the line provided. If the underlined word is spelled correctly, mark the box with an X.

Ronnie's TV

Mom <u>does'nt</u> want me to watch much TV. She says that two hours a day is plenty. We only have one TV in our house. It's in the <u>liveing</u> room. When I do get the chance to watch some TV, I have to share my time. After we finish our <u>homewurk</u>, my sister and I can't ever seem to agree on what to watch. We usually waste a least an hour <u>fliping</u> between different shows. After dinner, my parents like to watch the <u>evening</u> news. The news program lasts a half-hour. That only <u>leaveses</u> me with 30 minutes of television before I go to bed.

1. Mom <u>does'nt</u> want me to watch much TV.

   _____

   ☐ The word is spelled correctly as is.

2. It's in the <u>liveing</u> room.

   _____

   ☐ The word is spelled correctly as is.

3. After we finish our <u>homewurk</u>, my sister and I can't ever seem to agree on what to watch.

   _____

   ☐ The word is spelled correctly as is.

4. We usually waste a least an hour <u>fliping</u> between different shows.

_____

☐ The word is spelled correctly as is.

5. After dinner, my parents like to watch the <u>evening</u> news.

_____

☐ The word is spelled correctly as is.

6. That only <u>leaveses</u> me with 30 minutes of television before I go to bed.

_____

☐ The word is spelled correctly as is.

Directions: Punctuation and Capitalization—Use the selection to answer Questions 7–13. If what is <u>underlined</u> is not correct, either fill in the circle next to the correct answer or write it correctly on the line provided.

S-U-C-C-E-S-S

It was a Monday night. My eyes were fixed on the kitchen <u>table</u> A huge list of words was staring back at me. From <u>A to Z</u> there were at least 10 words for every letter. Some letters had 20 words <u>listed</u> These words were going to be asked at the spelling bee that I was preparing for. I was frustrated. I closed my eyes and put my head on the table. My Aunt Melinda felt sorry for me. She sat down beside me and rubbed my head. "Anything I can <u>do."</u> she asked. I showed her my list.

"You should be proud of yourself," <u>aunt melinda</u> said.

<u>   I</u> should?"

"Any kid who has even tried to learn these words is a success." She wrote the word success at the top of the page.   <u>"I</u> know you can do it. I'll help you practice for the spelling bee."

7. My eyes were fixed on the kitchen <u>table</u>

   ○ A. table!
   ○ B. table.
   ○ C. table;
   ○ D. Correct as is

8. From <u>A to Z</u> there were at least 10 words for every letter.

   ○ A. a to Z
   ○ B. A to z
   ○ C. a to z
   ○ D. Correct as is

9. Some letters had 20 words <u>listed</u>

   ○ A. listed,
   ○ B. listed:
   ○ C. listed.
   ○ D. Correct as is

10. "Anything I can <u>do."</u> she asked.

    ○ A. do,"
    ○ B. do?"
    ○ C. do?
    ○ D. Correct as is

11. "You should be proud of yourself," <u>aunt melinda</u> said.

    _____

    ☐ The words use correct capitalization as is.

12. <u>I</u> should?"

    ○ A. "I
    ○ B. 'I
    ○ C. "I'
    ○ D. Correct as is

13. <u>"I</u> know you can do it.

    ○ A. 'I
    ○ B. 'I"
    ○ C. I
    ○ D. Correct as is

Directions: Grammar and Usage Activities—Use the selection to answer Questions 14–20. If the <u>underlined</u> word is not correct, fill in the circle next to the correct answer.

What Does Buster Have to Say?

Last week, Buster <u>was</u> sitting at the edge of my bed. I leaned over to pet his black-and-white striped fur. Suddenly, the most amazing thing <u>happens</u>.

"I hate it when you tickle me, " Buster said. <u>It</u> stood up and moved away from my hand. With soft steps, he walked across the edge of <u>me</u> bed and made himself comfortable on a soft blanket. I couldn't believe it! Buster, my cat, was talking to me! I didn't know what to do; cats <u>ain't</u> supposed to talk.

"I <u>don't</u> like to be tickled. I also want you to know that I don't like the cat food in that blue bag. I like the stuff in the red bag. So tell Mom what to buy next time you're at the grocery store."

Then I felt Buster crawling around my legs. I <u>opened</u> my eyes and realized it was all a dream.

14. Last week, Buster <u>was</u> sitting at the edge of my bed.

   ○ A. were
   ○ B. is
   ○ C. did
   ○ D. Correct as is

15. Suddenly, the most amazing thing <u>happens</u>.

   ○ A. happened
   ○ B. is happening
   ○ C. did happen
   ○ D. Correct as is

16. <u>It</u> stood up and moved away from my hand.

   ○ A. She
   ○ B. He
   ○ C. They
   ○ D. Correct as is

17. With soft steps, he walked across the edge of <u>me</u> bed and made himself comfortable on a soft blanket.

    ○ A. his
    ○ B. mine
    ○ C. my
    ○ D. Correct as is

18. I didn't know what to do; cats <u>ain't</u> supposed to talk.

    ○ A. aren't
    ○ B. are'nt
    ○ C. can't
    ○ D. Correct as is

19. "I <u>don't</u> like to be tickled.

    ○ A. did not
    ○ B. does not
    ○ C. was not
    ○ D. Correct as is

20. I <u>opened</u> my eyes and realized it was all a dream.

    ○ A. did open
    ○ B. opens
    ○ C. will open
    ○ D. Correct as is

Reading

Introduction

In the Reading section of the Ohio Achievement Test (OAT), you will be asked questions to test what you have learned so far in school. These questions are based on the reading skills you have been taught in school through fourth grade. The questions you will answer are not meant to confuse or trick you but are written so you have the best chance to show what you know.

Questions I Will Answer on the OAT

You will answer multiple-choice, short-answer, and extended-response questions on the Reading OAT. Multiple-choice items have four answer choices, and only one is correct. Short-answer items will require you to write a word, a phrase, or a sentence. Extended-response items will require you to write a few phrases, or a complete sentence or two.

The questions are based on reading selections. The selections may be literary or expository. Literary selections are fiction. Expository selections are informative.

Examples of an expository selection, a multiple-choice item, a short-answer item, and an extended-response item are shown below.

The Narwhal

Narwhals are part of the whale family. They are white on the bottom and are gray on top. They have small, curved heads with bulbous foreheads. Their bodies are covered with dark brown spots. They have very small beaks and short flippers. Each narwhal has two teeth. The teeth of the female almost never grow beyond the gums. The male's right tooth usually doesn't grow, but the left tooth develops to become a tusk. In adult narwhal whales, the tusk can grow to a length of 1.5–3 meters (5–10 feet). This is more than half of the length of the narwhal's body. The tusk is very hard. It grows in a counterclockwise spiral and looks like a twisted walking stick.

1. According to the passage, how many tusks do narwhals have?

    ● A. one
    ○ B. two
    ○ C. three
    ○ D. four

2. List two physical characteristics of narwhals.

    1. short flippers
    2. very small beaks

3. Write one sentence to describe how the narwhal's tusk develops.

    The tusk starts as the left tooth of the male narwhal, and grows in a counterclockwise spiral.

Item Distribution on the OAT for Grade 4 Reading

Number of Items	36 or 37
Number of Multiple Choice Questions	29
Number of Short Answer Questions	4 or 6
Number of Extended-Response Questions	2 or 3
Types of Passages	2–3 Informational Texts 2–3 Literary Texts
Length of Passages	1 short (up to 300 words) 2 medium (301–500 words) 2 long (501–700 words)

Note: This is the Item Distribution that will be used on the actual OAT for Grade 4 Reading. Each practice test in this book contains 40 questions.

Scoring

The Reading questions are based on five reading selections. The selections may be literary or expository. Literary selections are fictional. Expository selections are informative.

You will answer multiple-choice, short-answer, and extended-response questions in the Reading OAT. Multiple-choice items have four answer choices, and only one is correct. Short-answer items will require you to write a word, a phrase, or a sentence. Extended-response items will require you to write a few phrases, or a complete sentence or two.

Multiple-Choice Items

Multiple-choice items are used whenever a single, concise answer to the item is possible. The multiple-choice questions on the OAT for Grade 4 Reading emphasize critical thinking over factual recollection. The multiple-choice items are worth one point each. There is no penalty for guessing; an item with no response will be automatically counted as incorrect.

Short-Answer and Extended-Response Items

Conventions of writing (sentence structure, word choice, usage, grammar, spelling, and mechanics) will not affect the scoring of short-answer and extended-response items unless there is interference with the clear communication of ideas.

Short-Answer Scoring

Short-answer items are scored on a 2-point scale. Here is a sample of a 2-point rubric:

A **2-point** response is complete and appropriate. It demonstrates a thorough understanding of the reading selection. It indicates logical reasoning and conclusions. It is accurate, relevant, comprehensive, and detailed.

A **1-point** response is partially appropriate. It contains minor flaws in reasoning or neglects to address some aspect of the item or question. It is mostly accurate and relevant but lacks comprehensiveness. It demonstrates an incomplete understanding of the reading selection or inability to make coherent meaning from the text.

A **Zero** is assigned if there is no response or if the response indicates no understanding of the reading selection or item.

A **NS (Non-Scorable)** is assigned if the response is unreadable, illegible, or written in a language other than English.

Extended-Response Scoring

Extended-response items will be scored on a 4-point scale. Here is a sample of a 4-point rubric:

A **4-point** response provides extensive evidence of the kind of interpretation called for in the item or question. The response is well-organized, elaborate, and thorough. It demonstrates a complete understanding of the whole work as well as how parts blend to form the whole. It is relevant, comprehensive, and detailed, demonstrating a thorough understanding of the reading selection. It thoroughly addresses the important elements of the question. It contains logical reasoning and communicates effectively and clearly.

A **3-point** response provides evidence that an essential interpretation has been made. It is thoughtful and reasonably accurate. It indicates an understanding of the concept or item, communicates adequately, and generally reaches reasonable conclusions. It contains some combination of the following flaws: minor flaws in reasoning or interpretation, failure to address some aspect of the item, or the omission of some detail.

A **2-point** response is mostly accurate and relevant. It contains some combination of the following flaws: incomplete evidence of interpretation, unsubstantial statements made about the text, an incomplete understanding of the concept or item, lack of comprehensiveness, faulty reasoning, and/or unclear communication.

A **1-point** response provides little evidence of interpretation. It is unorganized and incomplete. It exhibits decoding rather than reading. It demonstrates a partial understanding of the item but is sketchy and unclear. It indicates some effort beyond restating the item. It contains some combination of the following flaws: little understanding of the concept or item, failure to address most aspects of the item, or inability to make coherent meaning from text.

A **Zero** is assigned if the response shows no understanding of the item or if the student fails to respond to the item.

A **NS (Non-Scorable)** is assigned if the response is unreadable, illegible, or written in a language other than English.

Directions for Practice Test 1

This Grade 4 Reading Achievement Practice Test has 40 multiple-choice, short-answer, and extended-response questions. Read each selection carefully before you answer the questions.

There are several important things to remember as you take this test:
- Read each multiple-choice question carefully. Think about what is being asked. Then fill in one answer bubble to mark your answer.
- If you do not know the answer to a multiple-choice question, skip it and go on. If you have time, go back to the questions you skipped and answer them.
- For short-answer and extended-response questions, write your response clearly and neatly on the lines provided.
- If you finish the Practice Test early, go back and check over your work.

Go to next page

Directions: Read the selection.

The Narwhal

Narwhals are part of the whale family. They are white on the bottom and are gray on top. They have small, curved heads with bulbous foreheads. Their bodies are covered with dark brown spots. They have very small beaks and short flippers. Each narwhal has two teeth. The teeth of the female almost never grow beyond the gums. The male's right tooth usually doesn't grow, but the left tooth develops to become a tusk. In adult narwhal whales, the tusk can grow to a length of 1.5–3 meters (5–10 feet). This is more than half of the length of the narwhal's body. The tusk is very hard. It grows in a counterclockwise spiral and looks like a twisted walking stick.

Scientists have made many guesses about how the narwhal uses the long tusk. Some think it is used to poke animals on the ocean floor. Others think it is used to spear fish or to break holes in the ice that overlays the Arctic Ocean's surface. But these may not be correct hypotheses because the female narwhal, which has no tusk, survives just as well as the male. The narwhal, with its strange tusk, makes this type of whale one of the most recognized, but least understood, in the world.

Directions: Use the selection to answer questions 1–8.

1. But these may not be correct **hypotheses** because the female narwhal, which has no tusk, survives just as well as the male.

   What does **hypotheses** mean?

   ○ A. freak accidents
   ○ B. random thoughts
   ○ C. wild guesses
   ○ D. educated guesses

2. Read the dictionary definitions below for the word **develop**.

> **de•vel•op** (di vel´əp) *verb*
> **1.** to make a photograph using chemicals **2.** to make something better **3.** to grow **4.** to use land for a purpose

Which meaning best fits the way **develops** is used in the first paragraph?

○ A. Meaning 1

○ B. Meaning 2

○ C. Meaning 3

○ D. Meaning 4

3. They have small, curved heads with **bulbous** foreheads.

What does the word **bulbous** mean?

○ A. pointy

○ B. flat

○ C. rounded

○ D. giant

4. What does **overlays** mean, as used in the second paragraph of this selection?

○ A. covers

○ B. shows

○ C. folds

○ D. wraps

5. List two guesses scientists have about how the narwhal uses its tusk.

   _____

   _____

6. Where would you find additional information on narwhals?

   ○ A. in a book about marine life
   ○ B. in a magazine about wildlife in Africa
   ○ C. in an article about icebergs
   ○ D. in a web site about killer whales

7. What is the main idea of this selection?

   ○ A. Narwhals are considered part of the whale family.
   ○ B. Narwhals have a tusk used for stabbing animals.
   ○ C. Narwhals are very recognizable yet not completely understood.
   ○ D. Narwhals live in the Arctic Ocean.

8. Which of the following is NOT a trait shared by male and female narwhals?

   ○ A. a bulbous head
   ○ B. a long tusk
   ○ C. short flippers
   ○ D. bodies covered with dark brown spots

Go to next page

Directions: Read the selection.

Help Our Planet

Every day, we make trash. But have you ever stopped to think about what happens to that trash? What happens to the cereal box, the milk carton, or the soda cans? We live on a planet with limited resources. We need to think about how we use them.

If we just throw stuff away, the trash ends up at a dump. When trash dumps fill up, new ones have to be made. Sometimes trash is burned. Burning the trash also causes problems. It can make the air dirty. We need better ideas for dealing with trash. Think about a trash can overflowing with garbage; if we don't find an answer, someday our planet will be bursting with trash as well.

The best plan has three parts to it. First, we need to change the way we think. Buy things that have less packaging. Many things we buy now come in smaller packages with only one item in them. These are nice, but they make quite a bit of extra trash. We need to think about how much waste we are making every day.

Another step that reduces trash is reusing things. A milk carton could become a bird feeder. The bags that we normally throw away can be washed out and used again. Reusing things is a great way to help keep down the amount of trash we make.

The third step is recycling. Recycling is taking something and making a new thing from it using the same material. Glass, plastics, paper, and aluminum are all recyclable materials. Newspapers and magazines can be recycled. By recycling these things, you are beginning something important.

Recycling is very important. It saves the resources of our planet. People play the most important part in recycling because they decide what to buy and what to throw away. Every little bit helps when it comes to recycling. We all need to help make our planet a better place to live.

Directions: Use the selection to answer questions 9–16.

9. Think about a trash can **overflowing** with garbage; if we don't find an answer, someday our planet will be bursting with trash as well.

   What does the word **overflowing** mean?

   ○ A. not filled enough
   ○ B. halfway filled
   ○ C. empty
   ○ D. filled over the top

10. Which of the following sentences from the passage is a fact?

    ○ A. Recycling is very important.

    ○ B. We need to think about how much waste we are making every day.

    ○ C. Glass, plastics, paper, and aluminum are all recyclable materials.

    ○ D. We need better ideas for dealing with trash.

11. What is the main idea of this passage?

    ○ A. Many things people use around the house can be recycled.

    ○ B. People need to start finding ways to create less trash.

    ○ C. Plastic milk cartons make good bird feeders.

    ○ D. People should stop throwing away cereal boxes and soda cans.

12. In the second paragraph, what does the author mean by saying, "someday our planet will be bursting with trash as well"?

    ○ A. Our planet will explode because of trash.

    ○ B. Our planet will fall apart because there is too much trash on it.

    ○ C. There will be so much trash on the surface of our planet that it will look like an over-filled trash can.

    ○ D. Our planet will start shouting because it does not like being filled with trash.

13. Reusing things is a great way to help keep down the amount of trash we make.

    Which word lets you know this is an opinion?

    ○ A. great

    ○ B. amount

    ○ C. help

    ○ D. trash

14. List four items mentioned in the passage that are recyclable.

    1. _____

    2. _____

    3. _____

    4. _____

15. What is a negative effect of burning trash?

    ○ A. It eliminates trash.

    ○ B. It can make the air dirty.

    ○ C. It creates more trash that needs to be burned.

    ○ D. It emits a clean odor.

16. What would happen if people followed the suggestions presented in this article?

    ○ A. There would be more trash on the planet.

    ○ B. Companies would use more packaging for items.

    ○ C. There would be less pollution and the earth would be cleaner.

    ○ D. There would be a need for larger trash dumps.

Directions: Read the selection.

Sally's Summer Vacation

My summer vacation was GREAT! It was the best summer of my life. Early in the summer, new neighbors moved in next door. I wasn't sure this would be a good thing. Our old neighbors were very nice, but, when the new family introduced themselves, I met Lita. She's my age, and I couldn't have been happier!

For a best friend, Lita is really fun. She likes everything I like. She likes eating pizza, making popcorn, and watching movies in the movie theater again and again. She likes making cookies and decorating them with frosting, and so do I! She also likes to go swimming every day.

Because we like a lot of the same stuff, Lita and I hung out almost every day. I would go over to her house, or she would come over to my house. Some days, we would go to the pool; other days, we would ride our bikes to the neighborhood park.

I had to take a trip to my grandmother's house for a week, and I was lonely. I don't have any brothers or sisters to play with. I was glad to be home again to see Lita. It also made me happy that there were only a few days until school started. Lita isn't in my class at school this year, but that's OK. We're neighbors, and we'll get to walk to and from school together every day.

Doug's Summer Vacation

For my summer vacation, I didn't do very much. I played with my little brother during the day, and, sometimes, we watched TV together. He's pretty young, and he doesn't really like TV. He talks too much and makes noises. He likes to play with blocks. Usually, I build things so he can knock them over. I call him "Little Destroyer." He giggles and claps his hands.

We didn't go on any trips. My aunt came to visit us, but she didn't want to play video games with me. She said she didn't know how. I offered to teach her, but she was too busy. She did make some good brownies, though.

When it was hot outside, I sat in my brother's wading pool. Even though it doesn't hold much water, it was enough to keep me cool. I hooked up the hose a few times and ran through the sprinkler. My little brother would laugh when the water hit his toes. Once or twice, I went to the public pool. Most days, I rode my bike through the neighborhood, alone. There aren't many kids in my neighborhood. I'm glad school has started again.

Go to next page

Directions: Use the selection to answer questions 17–24.

17. When it was hot outside, I sat in my brother's **wading pool**.

    A **wading pool** is

    ○ A. a deep pool of water.

    ○ B. a shallow pool of water.

    ○ C. a pool the size of a large lake.

    ○ D. an empty pool.

18. How is Sally's summer vacation different from Doug's summer vacation?

    ○ A. Sally goes to the pool; Doug does not.

    ○ B. Doug rides his bike; Sally does not ride her bike.

    ○ C. Doug spends time at his aunt's house; Sally never visits anyone.

    ○ D. Sally hangs out with someone her own age; Doug does not.

19. What is one reason Doug is happy for school to start again?

    ○ A. There aren't many kids in his neighborhood for him to hang out with.

    ○ B. His best friend is not in his class at school this year.

    ○ C. He is tired of his brother knocking things over.

    ○ D. He is tired of playing video games.

20. How would the passage "Doug's Summer Vacation" be different if it took place in a setting where the weather is cold?

    ○ A. Doug probably would not play as many video games.

    ○ B. Doug probably would not watch TV with his brother.

    ○ C. Doug probably would not make brownies with his aunt.

    ○ D. Doug probably would not run through the sprinkler.

21. How are the main characters in the two passages different?

    ○ A. Sally has a younger brother, and Doug does not have a brother.

    ○ B. Sally has an older sister, and Doug has a younger sister.

    ○ C. Doug has a younger brother, and Sally does not have a brother.

    ○ D. Doug has an older sister, and Sally has a younger sister.

22. How does the theme of "Sally's Summer Vacation" compare with the theme of "Doug's Summer Vacation"?

    ○ A. "Sally's Summer Vacation" is about a fun summer vacation; "Doug's Summer Vacation" is about a not-so-fun summer vacation.

    ○ B. "Doug's Summer Vacation" is about a fun summer vacation; "Sally's Summer Vacation" is about a not-so-fun summer vacation.

    ○ C. Both stories are about not-so-fun summer vacations.

    ○ D. Both stories are about fun summer vacations.

23. How would Sally's summer most likely be different if she spends the whole summer at her grandmother's house?

    ○ A. She would not be able to play with her sister.

    ○ B. She would not be able to eat pizza.

    ○ C. She would not spend time with her new neighbor, Lita.

    ○ D. She would not be able to watch movies.

24. Which of the following lets the reader know Sally probably enjoys doing things outside?

    ○ A. She and Lita liked to watch movies and decorate cookies.

    ○ B. She and Lita often went to the pool and rode their bikes in the park.

    ○ C. She spent most of the trip to her grandmother's playing outside.

    ○ D. She spent most of the summer with her friend Lita.

A Knight's Feast

A tall boy of 10 years, Arthur sat stiffly behind his father on the horse that was carrying them to the castle of the king. Arthur had never been to the castle, but it was time for him to learn the ways of the knights. Arthur's father was a knight, and, as they rode, his father's protective armor clinked and clanked. The armor was heavy, too heavy for Arthur to wear. The helmet alone weighed nearly 40 pounds. Arthur couldn't wait for the day when he too would be able to wear knight's armor and serve the king.

The journey would take Arthur and his father to the king's castle for a feast. Arthur was amazed by all he saw on his journey: fellow travelers, tall trees, and small cottages. He had never traveled far from home before. But, when the two came upon the castle, Arthur shut his eyes tight. They slowly crossed a drawbridge, which stood over a deep moat. The water below made Arthur nervous. Someone had once told him crocodiles and snakes lived in these deep pits. He held his breath until the horse reached the castle's huge gates.

Upon opening his eyes, Arthur saw a windmill within the castle walls. His father directed the horse to a small stable. When Arthur's feet hit the ground, he could hardly keep them still. He couldn't wait to see the world inside the castle walls. As they made their way to the king's feast, Arthur and his father passed the hawk house. The hawks were birds trained to hunt small animals inside the castle, his father explained. They passed people selling fruits from carts and musicians who filled the air with beautiful music. Before long, Arthur could hear voices echoing inside the Great Hall. The feast was just beginning.

Arthur's eyes were wide with amazement as he took in all the sights. The smells of the feast were wonderful. A group of men was standing near the door with horns and drums. Trays of food were being carried in front of Arthur as he stood in his father's shadow.

There were fireplaces at both ends of the Great Hall. Beautiful paintings and rugs hung from every inch of the room's large walls. Arthur had never seen so many people before. Men and women, dressed in capes and long dresses, walked through the room and sat together at long, wooden tables. Entertainers in brightly colored clothes went through the crowd, some juggling, some singing, some telling tales.

Arthur's father led him to a table where the king sat among a large group of people.

"So what do you think of my feast?" the king asked Arthur. He had the loudest voice Arthur had ever heard—it sounded like thunder.

Nervous, Arthur shook his head. He wanted to say something nice, but his tongue was in knots.

"Yes, your feast is wonderful," Arthur managed to say, but the king was already speaking with someone else.

"You speak to the king when he addresses you," said his father. "You want to be a knight, don't you?"

Arthur agreed.

"You'll have another chance tomorrow. That's when the king watches the knights practice."

Arthur took a seat at one of the wooden tables. He felt something warm and furry brush against his leg. He looked under the table and saw two dogs happily chewing on bones. Arthur gave the closer dog a short pat on the head.

"I'll get him tomorrow," Arthur whispered.

Directions: Use the selection to answer questions 25–32.

25. In the fourth paragraph, when Arthur's eyes are wide with amazement, Arthur looks

    ○ A. surprised.
    ○ B. scared.
    ○ C. angry.
    ○ D. sad.

26. When the king asks Arthur about the feast, why doesn't Arthur answer right away?

    ○ A. Arthur doesn't like the feast.
    ○ B. Arthur's father doesn't want Arthur to answer.
    ○ C. It is too loud inside the castle, and Arthur doesn't hear the king.
    ○ D. Arthur is too nervous to speak.

27. What would Arthur probably do if he saw a snake in the moat?

    ○ A. He would show fear.
    ○ B. He would want to keep the snake as a pet.
    ○ C. He would not do anything.
    ○ D. He would bring everyone else to see the snake.

28. Read the first sentence of the summary.

    Arthur is a young boy whose father is taking him to meet the king.

    Which of the following best completes the summary?

    ○ A. Arthur has to close his eyes because he is afraid of the creatures in the moat. When Arthur gets to the castle, he sees many people and things he has never seen before.

    ○ B. Arthur sees many things such as travelers and cottages on his way to the castle. While he is at the feast, Arthur feels something furry under the table. He looks under the table and finds two dogs.

    ○ C. Arthur's father is taking him to the castle so Arthur can learn to be a knight. At first, Arthur is too nervous to speak to the king, but he thinks he will do better the next day.

    ○ D. When Arthur and his father get to the castle, they put their horse in a small stable. On their way to the feast, they pass many merchants and musicians. They reach the Great Hall at the beginning of the feast.

29. How does Arthur feel about being inside the castle?

    ○ A. He is afraid of the new people.
    ○ B. He is curious about everything.
    ○ C. He is happy to see his old friends at the castle.
    ○ D. He is angry because he wasn't invited to the feast.

30. Why are Arthur and his father traveling to the king's feast?

    ○ A. Arthur is old enough to learn the ways of the knights.
    ○ B. Arthur and his father are hungry.
    ○ C. Arthur's father is being honored by the king.
    ○ D. Arthur has been chosen by the king to become a knight.

31. What will Arthur most likely do the next day?

    ○ A. Arthur will go home.
    ○ B. Arthur will ignore the king.
    ○ C. Arthur will ignore his father.
    ○ D. Arthur will speak to the king.

32. List two things Arthur saw on his journey to the king's castle for the feast.

    1. _____

    _____

    2. _____

    _____

Go to next page ➡

Directions: Read the selection.

Lightning Safety

Lightning is an extremely dangerous weather event. Lightning is a big charge of electricity that can reach from clouds to the ground or to other clouds. It can start fires and it is strong enough to hurt or kill people. There are thousands of lightning strikes every day. Every year, about 100 people are killed by lightning in the United States.

Lightning can strike as far as 10 miles away from a storm. Lightning can strike anywhere in a big circle around where the rain is falling. Sometimes you can feel when lightning might be about to strike. Try holding your arm very close to the front of a color TV screen that is turned on and see how it feels. Look at the hair standing up on your arm. If you are in or near a storm and you feel this way, then you may be in danger.

Lightning could strike at any second. If you are outside and you see lightning in the sky, get inside your house or another building as quickly as possible. If you're in an open field or a yard, look for a low place to lie in. If you're in the mountains or woods, try to find a cave to stay in until the storm passes. If you can't find any shelter, get as close to the ground as possible.

Another safe place to be during a thunderstorm is a metal vehicle, like a car or truck. All windows should be closed. Do not touch anything inside the car or truck that is made of metal, such as a doorknob. Note that some cars are not made of metal. In this case, it is not as safe as a metal car when there is lightning in the sky.

When you stand out in the open during a thunderstorm, your body is like a lightning rod. A lightning rod is a tall, metal pole that is placed on a building, such as a house. One end of the lightning rod is placed in the ground. When lightning strikes a lightning rod, the electricity goes into the ground and away from the building. Lightning tends to strike the highest thing it is near. If you stand in an open field, you're likely to be the tallest thing in the vicinity, and you put yourself at risk.

Trees can also attract lightning. Think about their heights. In many cases, trees are the tallest things around. It's no wonder they are often hit by lightning. For this reason, never stand under a tree during a thunderstorm.

Another place to stay away from during a lightning storm is the water. Water is a conductor of electricity. This means electricity passes through it easily. Get out of the water at the first sign of lightning. If you are out on a boat, get to shore and off the boat as soon as you can.

There are other things you should stay away from when you see lightning. Put down your fishing pole and metal sports gear, including baseball or softball bats and golf clubs. You do not want to be holding a metal rod in your hand if lightning strikes; this is true for metal umbrellas as well.

Go to next page

Directions: Use the selection to answer questions 33–40.

33. If you stand in an open field, you're likely to be the tallest thing in the **vicinity**, and you put yourself at risk.

    What does **vicinity** mean?

    ○ A. place
    ○ B. water
    ○ C. avoid
    ○ D. tree

34. Why would it be important to stay away from a lake or a river during a thunderstorm?

    ○ A. Water can be compared to a lightning rod.
    ○ B. It is best to be outside during a thunderstorm.
    ○ C. Electricity passes easily through water.
    ○ D. It is hard to get to shore during a thunderstorm.

35. What is the main idea of the sixth paragraph?

    ○ A. It is good to stand near a tree during a thunderstorm.
    ○ B. Because they are tall, trees attract lightning during a thunderstorm.
    ○ C. People should think about the heights of trees during a thunderstorm.
    ○ D. It is better to stand near a tree than near water during a thunderstorm.

36. Which sentence from the passage tells you why it would be best to carry a plastic umbrella during a thunderstorm?

    ○ A. "Lightning tends to strike the highest thing it is near."
    ○ B. "If you are outside and you see lightning in the sky, get inside your house or another building as quickly as possible."
    ○ C. "Another safe place to be during a thunderstorm is a metal vehicle, like a car or truck."
    ○ D. "You do not want to be holding a metal rod in your hand if lightning strikes; this is true for metal umbrellas as well."

Go to next page

37. Look at this diagram of information from the article.

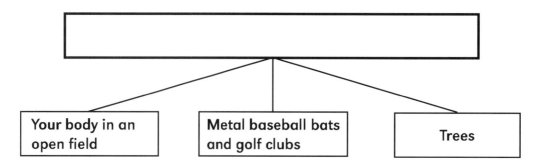

Which idea belongs in the empty box?

- A. How to stay safe during a thunderstorm
- B. Things that can act as lightning rods
- C. Things to carry during a thunderstorm
- D. Why lightning is attracted to lightning rods

38. What does the word **extremely** mean as it is used in the first paragraph?

- A. sort of
- B. hardly
- C. closely
- D. very

39. Which of these would be the safest place to be during a thunderstorm?

- A. a cave in the woods
- B. a car with open windows
- C. a field with many trees
- D. a baseball field

40. What is lightning? Why is it dangerous?

_____

_____

_____

_____

Directions for Practice Test 2

This Grade 4 Reading Achievement Practice Test has 40 multiple-choice, short-answer, and extended-response questions. Read each selection carefully before you answer the questions.

There are several important things to remember as you take this test:
- Read each multiple-choice question carefully. Think about what is being asked. Then fill in one answer bubble to mark your answer.
- If you do not know the answer to a multiple-choice question, skip it and go on. If you have time, go back to the questions you skipped and answer them.
- For short-answer and extended-response questions, write your response clearly and neatly on the lines provided.
- If you finish the Practice Test early, go back and check over your work.

Directions: Read the selection.

The Big Hit

Kylie loved baseball. From the minute she got up in the morning to the time she closed her eyes at night, Kylie thought about baseball. Sometimes, this got her into trouble, like at school. Her fourth-grade teacher didn't like daydreamers, but that was all Kylie wanted to do.

"Kylie, if only you knew your multiplication tables like you know about your favorite baseball players," Mrs. Cooper would sigh as she returned Kylie's math test.

Kylie wasn't a very good student. Her mind always seemed to wander when she sat down to do school work. Kylie wasn't a very good baseball player, either. But, unlike homework, baseball was something Kylie was **passionate** about, and she practiced every chance she could get.

Kylie went to the park every afternoon and hung around the batting cages where the town's best baseball players went to practice. Usually, if she waited long enough, someone would pitch a few to her, but Kylie never hit the ball. No matter how **frequently** she practiced, no matter how hard she tried to hit the ball, it never happened.

One Friday, Kylie was standing behind the cages when a batter she had never seen before caught her eye. She watched him closely. Kylie studied how he stretched, how he pulled his glove out of his bag and checked it over, and how he took his bat out and ran his hands up and down, checking every inch for dings or dents. Kylie wanted to learn all the secrets of baseball. Suddenly, the batter seemed to notice Kylie was watching him.

"I'm Scott. Want me to pitch some to you?" he asked Kylie.

Kylie was so excited that she could hardly answer, "Sure."

Kylie grabbed her bat. Scott pitched once, then again, and then again. With each pitch, Kylie swung into the air without a hit.

Scott stopped. He looked at Kylie for a minute.

"Can you see the ball?" he asked, walking toward her. Kylie was embarrassed. She hung her head and didn't answer.

"Here," Scott said, as he held out his hand. Kylie looked up slowly. He was holding out a pair of glasses. Kylie **appeared** to be confused.

"Put these on." The glasses were heavy and too big for her eyes, but Kylie looked through the lenses to see that everything was clear.

Go to next page

Scott stepped back and pitched again. Kylie swung the bat and missed. She hung her head.

"One more," Scott said. So Kylie got ready, with the large glasses sitting on her nose. She swung at the pitch, and, for the first time in her life, Kylie hit the ball.

Word Bank
passionate— to care a lot about something
frequently— to do something often, like practice sports
appeared— to seem a certain way, such as happy or sad

Directions: Use the selection to answer questions 1–8.

1. What is one reason Kylie has a hard time hitting a baseball?

    ○ A. She is afraid of the ball.

    ○ B. She cannot throw very well.

    ○ C. She cannot see the ball.

    ○ D. She does not have the right type of bat.

2. Which of the following lets the reader know Kylie wants to improve at baseball?

    ○ A. Her mind wanders when she does her homework.

    ○ B. She visits the batting cages and studies the batters.

    ○ C. She asks her mom for a pair of glasses so she can see the ball.

    ○ D. She plays on a baseball team.

3. What would most likely be different about this story if it took place on a playground?

    ○ A. Kylie would probably not daydream as much in school.

    ○ B. Kylie would probably be able to hit the ball better than she does at the batting cages.

    ○ C. Kylie would probably find more people to pitch to her than she does at the batting cages.

    ○ D. Kylie would probably not be able to find as many batters to watch as she does at the batting cages.

Go to next page

4. Why is Kylie finally able to hit the ball?

    ○ A. Scott lets Kylie borrow his bat.

    ○ B. Scott lets Kylie borrow a pair of glasses.

    ○ C. Scott is a better pitcher than the people who usually pitch to Kylie.

    ○ D. Scott tells Kylie the best way to hit a baseball.

5. What are two things Kylie learns while standing behind the batting cages watching Scott?

    1. _____

    2. _____

6. How do Scott and Kylie act when they're together?

    ○ A. Scott is mean and unhelpful toward Kylie.

    ○ B. Kylie ignores Scott's suggestions on how she can become a better baseball player.

    ○ C. Scott realizes that there's nothing he can do to help Kylie.

    ○ D. Kylie accepts Scott's help so she can become a better baseball player.

7. Why isn't Kylie a good student?

    _____

    _____

8. How does the author's descriptions explain how Kylie feels about school?

    ○ A. The author uses words that make the reader think Kylie enjoys school.

    ○ B. The author uses words that make the reader think Kylie absolutely hates school.

    ○ C. The author uses words that make the reader think Kylie doesn't concentrate during school.

    ○ D. The author uses words that make the reader think Kylie is failing school.

Go to next page ➡

Directions: Read the selection.

Moving Up Day
By Pilar Diaz

My fellow fourth graders, it is with both sadness and happiness that I stand before you today on this Moving Up Day. In September, we become fifth graders. This is a move we should all be looking forward to because next year should be an exciting one.

We will always remember the first day of kindergarten. Most of us were scared. I think Billy Horton cried. Mrs. Alexander taught us to share, to sing and play games, to say our ABCs, and to count to 100 by 5s. We learned where the cafeteria and the library are. I remember how much I liked drinking milk out of that small box for the first time. Back then, we were the babies of the school. We had a lot to learn.

First grade came, and we started reading. We learned to add and subtract. We also started writing in our journals. My first page says, "I read a book today. It was fun. It was about rabbits." I'm sure glad I've improved since then. In first grade, we learned Thursdays were pizza days. I won't forget hanging upside down on the monkey bars at recess.

Second grade brought a new adventure—music class. I tried to play the piano. Mrs. Grant was patient, but I was not. We learned about dinosaurs and Earth and about rocket ships and the moon. I wrote all kinds of science facts in my journal. I remember something about nouns and verbs, too, but the other stuff is more exciting.

By third grade, we could use the classroom computers by ourselves. We used cursive writing and learned to multiply and divide. Gym class was filled with kickball and soccer.

And here we are, in fourth grade. There are so many memories; I can't talk about them all. It has been our best year, but it has also been the hardest. We've had really difficult history tests. Our science fair projects took six weeks. But the hardest part about fourth grade has been knowing that next year will be our last at Washington. How will I feel next year? I guess that's why they call it Moving Up Day, but maybe it should be called Moving On Day.

Announcement From Principal Vargas

To the fourth graders of Washington Elementary School:

Next year will be an important and exciting year for each of you. You are moving up to your last year at this school. There are many fun and wonderful things planned for you to do next year, but you will also have a lot of responsibility.

As the oldest in the school, you will be expected to help with the younger students. If they are lost, help them find their way to where they need to be. If they need help with schoolwork, use what you have learned here at school to help them. Knowledge is most exciting when you can share it with others.

Although we expect hard work and responsibility from you in the fifth grade, there will be fun times, too. As fifth graders, you will have work that will be different and more interesting than any you have had before. Our goal is to move you beyond work sheets and book reports; we want

Go to next page

to give you projects in which you have to work with others and think more creatively. The work you do next year will be hard, but I think you will find it interesting as well.

Enjoy your summer vacations. Have fun and spend a few months not thinking about school. But don't forget to read a few books and keep your minds from going to waste. Many changes and challenges await you in the fall.

Directions: Use the selection to answer questions 9–18.

9. According to Pilar Diaz, what happened in third grade?

   ○ A. The students learned to multiply and divide.
   ○ B. The students learned where the cafeteria and the library are.
   ○ C. The students started writing in journals.
   ○ D. The students learned to add and subtract.

10. Write one sentence that explains one of the responsibilities Principal Vargas tells the students they will have in fifth grade.

    _____

    _____

11. How does Pilar Diaz's speech compare with Principal Vargas' message?

    ○ A. Both talk about things that happened to the fourth graders in the past.
    ○ B. Both talk about what will happen to the fourth graders in the future.
    ○ C. Pilar Diaz talks about what happened to the fourth graders in the past; Principal Vargas talks about what will happen to them in the future.
    ○ D. Pilar Diaz talks about what will happen to the fourth graders in the future; Principal Vargas talks about what happened to them in the past.

12. What is one similar opinion that Pilar Diaz and Principal Vargas give in their speeches?

    ○ A. Both think fourth grade has been the hardest year for these students.
    ○ B. Both think the students are going to have a lot of responsibility next year.
    ○ C. Both think Moving Up Day should be called Moving On Day.
    ○ D. Both think the next year will be an exciting one for these students.

Go to next page ⟶

13. Look at the chart comparing information from the selection "Moving Up Day."

Kindergarten	
• Learned to share • Learned to sing and play games • Learned to say ABCs	• Started music class • Learned about the moon • Learned nouns and verbs

Which header belongs in the empty box?

○ A. First Grade

○ B. Second Grade

○ C. Third Grade

○ D. Fourth Grade

14. Look at this diagram of information from the selection "Announcement From Principal Vargas."

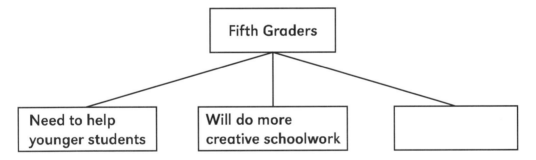

Which information belongs in the blank?

○ A. Will face many challenges in the fall

○ B. Might get lost in the school

○ C. Expect hard work from the students

○ D. Are planning fun things for next year

15. The work you do next year will be **hard**, but I think you will find it interesting as well.

    Which of the following words would be a good synonym to use in place of the word **hard**?

    ○ A. solid
    ○ B. difficult
    ○ C. simple
    ○ D. loud

16. How do you think Pilar Diaz will react as a fifth grader? Do you think she will enjoy her last year at Washington Elementary School? Why or why not?

    _____

    _____

    _____

    _____

17. What grade were Pilar and her classmates in when they were allowed to use the classroom computers by themselves?

    ○ A. second
    ○ B. third
    ○ C. fourth
    ○ D. fifth

18. What does the phrase "keep your minds from going to waste" mean?

    ○ A. Don't throw your brains in the garbage.
    ○ B. Don't be lazy and forget all the skills you have learned in school.
    ○ C. Don't lose your mind by reading scary books.
    ○ D. Don't have any fun during the summer.

Go to next page

Directions: Read the selection.

Lizard Madness

Max loved visiting his friend Jack, who lived near the ocean. The first afternoon after Max arrived, they saw two lizards scurrying up the side of the house. As quickly as they could, the two boys went toward the lizards and caught them. Holding the lizards in their hands, the boys went inside to ask Jack's mom for something to keep the lizards in. She found a small aquarium in the garage. The two boys stretched a window screen over the top of the tank. Then they went to get some sticks, leaves, grass, and sand to put in the tank to make the lizards feel more at home.

They put a small rounded shell in the bottom of the tank and filled it with water. They weren't sure what to feed the lizards. Jack called his friend, Carson, who owned a pet store.

Carson told the boys that they had caught salamanders, not lizards. The salamanders were coldblooded, he said, meaning their body temperature depends on their setting. While it was OK for the boys to keep them for a short time during the summer months, it wasn't a good idea to keep them when it started to get cold. Carson also said that salamanders need to be sprayed with water every now and then. This helps them and the things in their habitat stay wet. He let them know that salamanders eat mostly worms and insects.

The boys thanked Carson. Then, they went out to catch some bugs and worms to put in the cage with the salamanders. They also asked Jack's mom for a small bottle to spray water into the tank. Keeping a salamander would be a lot of hard work.

Directions: Use the selection to answer questions 19–24.

19. Why do the boys need a bottle to spray water into the tank?

    ○ A. Jack's mom tells the boys to keep the salamanders wet.

    ○ B. The boys know salamanders need liquid to drink.

    ○ C. Carson tells the boys to spray the salamanders to keep them moist.

    ○ D. The boys want to help the salamanders cool off.

20. Why is it important for the boys to know that salamanders are coldblooded?

    ○ A. The boys need to know how long to keep the salamanders.

    ○ B. The boys need to what is best for the salamanders.

    ○ C. The boys need to know what type of food the salamanders eat.

    ○ D. The boys need to know whether the salamanders are male or female.

Go to next page

21. Which of the following is the best summary of the passage?

    ○ A. Two boys find two lizards at the side of a house one afternoon. They catch both of the lizards and show them to one boy's mom. The boys find a tank to put the lizards in, and they give the lizards water, leaves, and grass.

    ○ B. Two boys find two animals one afternoon and decide to keep them. They call a pet store owner and find out that the animals are salamanders. The pet store owner tells them salamanders are coldblooded, and the boys realize that caring for salamanders would require a lot of work.

    ○ C. Two boys like to go out exploring in the woods. They also like to ride their bikes to the ocean. One day, they find two salamanders and keep them in a tank. A pet store owner tells the boys to feed the salamanders bugs and worms.

    ○ D. Two boys find a window screen in a garage. They put the screen over the top of a tank that had salamanders in it. They put water, sticks, leaves, grass, and sand in the tank and put the tank in a shaded place to keep it cool.

22. List four items the boys needed to put in the tank once they caught the salamanders.

    1. _____

    2. _____

    3. _____

    4. _____

23. How might this selection be different if Max and Jack were in the desert?

    ○ A. They could have caught fish instead of salamanders.
    ○ B. They could have caught frogs instead of salamanders.
    ○ C. They could have caught snakes instead of salamanders.
    ○ D. They could have caught toads instead of salamanders.

24. What does **coldblooded** mean?

    ○ A. body temperature is always cold
    ○ B. body temperature is never cold
    ○ C. body temperature is always hot
    ○ D. body temperature depends on the temperature of the setting

Go to next page

Directions: Read the selection.

Pinnipeds

Seals are animals in the pinniped family. Pinnipeds live both on land and in the sea. They generally leave the water and go onto land in order to mate, rest, give birth, or molt their fur. They use flippers to move. Seals move very easily in the water but have a harder time on land. On land, some seals move on all four flippers. Others use their front flippers and their stomach muscles to move themselves along. Most seals live in the salt-water oceans, but a few kinds live in fresh water. Seals are found along the coast and on islands. There are two kinds of seals: seals with ears (eared) and seals without ears (earless) seals.

Fur seals and sea lions are eared seals. They are called eared seals because they have ear flaps, which look like tiny ears that cover their ear holes. These seals can use all four flippers to walk on land because they can turn their back flippers forward and down. These seals use only their front flippers to swim, however. Sea lions are usually larger than fur seals. Sea lions move around easily on land and can travel far from the shore.

Fur seals have a heavy fur coat to keep them warm in the cold in which they live, and sea lions have blubber to keep them warm. This layer of blubber also helps them have a good shape for swimming. Because of this, they are able to chase their prey underwater easily so they can eat. Seals and sea lions eat a wide variety of food, including fish, squid, and mollusks.

Earless seals, such as the gray seal and the elephant seal, have excellent hearing. They hear well both in the water and out. They do, in fact, have ears, but they do not have ear flaps. Earless seals use their back flippers to swim, but they cannot use their back flippers to walk on land. They use their front flippers and bunch up their stomach muscles to move along, like a caterpillar moves.

All seals mate and have their babies in places called rookeries. Sea lion rookeries are on the sandy or rocky beaches of islands. Seal rookeries can be on islands also, but just as often they are on coasts. Sea lion babies, called pups, have brown fur, and fur seal pups have black fur. The fur of many earless seals is white or gray.

When babies are born, it is important that they are protected. Pinnipeds have few natural predators. Killer whales, some types of sharks, polar bears, and humans are the main predators. Seals and sea lions used to be hunted because early explorers would use their blubber for warmth and sell the fur for money and goods. Other threats that seals and sea lions face daily are water pollution and becoming entangled in fishing nets and trash in the oceans. Humans can help protect seals and sea lions by keeping the waters clean and helping rescue seals and sea lions that are caught in nets. The well-being of seals and sea lions not only shows care and concern for the animals, but also for the environment.

Go to next page

Directions: Use the selection to answer questions 25–34.

25. The author organizes the second and third paragraphs of the article by

    ○ A. telling about the life of a seal from birth to adulthood.

    ○ B. comparing and contrasting different types of seals.

    ○ C. describing how a sea lion walks on land.

    ○ D. explaining the problems of an earless seal.

26. What does the author tell you is the same about all the animals in this article?

    ○ A. They all have ear flaps.

    ○ B. They all have gray fur.

    ○ C. They all live on islands.

    ○ D. They all have flippers.

27. Other threats that seals and sea lions face daily are water pollution and becoming **entangled** in fishing nets and trash in the oceans.

    What does the word **entangled** mean?

    ○ A. caught

    ○ B. wet

    ○ C. cold

    ○ D. hungry

28. Because of this, they are able to chase their **prey** underwater easily so they can eat.

    What is a synonym for the word **prey**?

    ○ A. water

    ○ B. food

    ○ C. pray

    ○ D. plants

29. List two reasons that seals and sea lions used to be hunted.

    1._____

    2._____

30. Which of the following is NOT a threat to seals and sea lions?

    ○ A. water pollution

    ○ B. polar bears

    ○ C. rookeries

    ○ D. killer whales

31. According to the article, what is one thing that humans can do to help protect seals and sea lions?

    _____

    _____

    _____

    _____

32. How are fur seals and sea lions different?

    ○ A. Sea lions don't have ear flaps; fur seals do have ear flaps.

    ○ B. Sea lions are larger than fur seals.

    ○ C. Sea lions use their front flippers to swim; fur seals use their back flippers to swim.

    ○ D. Sea lions have fur to keep them warm; fur seals have blubber to keep them warm.

33. Which of the following is NOT something that seals and sea lions eat, according to the article?

    ○ A. squid

    ○ B. seaweed

    ○ C. clams

    ○ D. fish

34. How do earless seals swim?

    ○ A. They use only their front flippers.

    ○ B. They use only their back flippers.

    ○ C. They use both their front and back flippers.

    ○ D. They cannot swim.

Directions: Read the selection.

New York

The state of New York touches the waters of Lake Erie and Lake Ontario, two of the Great Lakes, and the Atlantic coast. New York also touches Canada and the U.S. states of Vermont, Massachusetts, Connecticut, Pennsylvania, and New Jersey.

New York was one of the original thirteen colonies and is rich with history. You can visit the Women's Rights National Historical Park, in Seneca Falls, or Fort Ticonderoga, where the first American victory in the Revolutionary War took place. On Ellis Island, you can learn about the many people who came to the United States from other countries over the years. Those people are called immigrants. Ellis Island was the first place they stopped when they came to America by boat.

New York State is home to the largest city in the United States: New York City. New York City is important to the United States as well as to other countries around the world. It is home to the United Nations. The United Nations is a group of countries who work for world peace and cooperation. New York City is also known for the many companies, businesses, and banks that are there. New York City is also home to Broadway, which is a street that has many theaters for plays and musicals. Radio City Music Hall and Carnegie Hall are both in New York City.

New York City is proud of its many people who live in more than 400 neighborhoods. It is also proud of its hundreds of tall buildings and its many interesting places.

Although New York City is the largest city in the state, Albany is the capital city. Albany rests in the eastern part of the state, along the Hudson River. Albany is quite different from New York City. Albany is much smaller. Also, government is more important than business in Albany.

Overall, the state of New York is a popular place for visitors from across the country and around the world. If you want to see a big city or visit historic places, New York is a state that has it all.

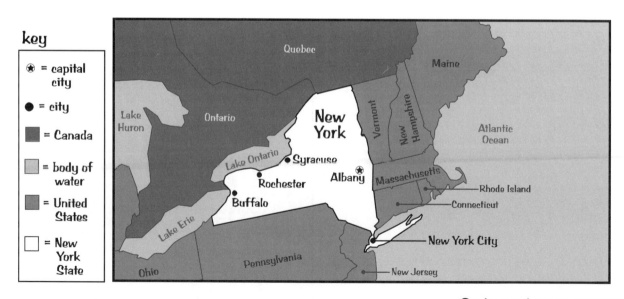

Go to next page ➡

Directions: Use the selection to answer questions 35–40.

35. What can visitors learn about at the museum on Ellis Island?

    ○ A. soldiers
    ○ B. women's rights
    ○ C. immigrants
    ○ D. world peace

36. The United Nations is a group of countries who work for world peace and **cooperation**.

    What does the word **cooperation** mean?

    ○ A. working against
    ○ B. working together
    ○ C. working alone
    ○ D. working separately

37. What can the reader tell about New York City from this passage?

    ○ A. There are not many tall buildings there.
    ○ B. Not many people work in offices there.
    ○ C. It costs a lot of money to move there.
    ○ D. People from many different backgrounds live there.

38. What is the state capital of New York?

    ○ A. New York City
    ○ B. Ellis Island
    ○ C. Albany
    ○ D. United Nations

39. Read the dictionary definitions below for the word **rich**.

> **rich** (rich) *adjective*
> **1.** having a great deal of money
> **2.** having a very heavy or sweet taste **3.** having a warm, strong color **4.** having a large supply

Which meaning best fits the way **rich** is used in the second paragraph?

○ A. Meaning 1
○ B. Meaning 2
○ C. Meaning 3
○ D. Meaning 4

40. Write one sentence to explain why you think New York State would be an interesting place to visit.

_____

_____

Mathematics

Introduction

In the Mathematics section of the Ohio Achievement Test (OAT), you will be asked questions to test what you have learned so far in school. These questions are based on the mathematics skills you have been taught in school through fourth grade. The questions you will answer are not meant to confuse or trick you but are written so you have the best chance to show what you know.

Questions I Will Answer on the OAT

You will answer multiple-choice, short-answer, and extended-response questions on the Mathematics OAT. Multiple-choice items have four answer choices, and only one is correct. Short-answer items will require you to write a word, a phrase, or a number sentence. Extended-response items will require you to write a few phrases, a complete sentence or two, or to show your work toward a numeric answer.

Examples of a multiple-choice item, a short-answer item, and an extended-response item are shown below.

1. Waldo wants to set a world record for spitting watermelon seeds the farthest. Right now, he can spit a watermelon seed 133 inches. The world record is 7 feet more than 711 inches. How many more inches does Waldo need to be able to spit a watermelon seed to be able to equal the record?

    ○ A. 578 inches

    ● B. 662 inches

    ○ C. 795 inches

    ○ D. 844 inches

2. Conchita has 29 hair ribbons. Her sister, Gretchen, has 13 hair ribbons. Write a number sentence that could be used to find how many hair ribbons the sisters have in total.

    29 + 13 = 42 hair ribbons

3. At the local pizza parlor, pizza costs $2.00 per slice, and $12.00 for a whole pie. How many slices of pizza are in one pie? How many pieces of pizza could you buy if you had $18.00?

    I would divide $12.00 by $2.00 to find how many pieces of pizza are in one pie, which equals 6. If I had $18.00 to spend on pizza, I would divide $18.00 by $2.00 to find how many pieces I could buy, which equals 9.

Item Distribution on the OAT for Grade 4 Mathematics

Number of Items	40
Number of Multiple-Choice	32
Number of Short-Answer	6
Number of Extended-Response	2
Number of Points	52

Scoring

Three types of items are used on the OAT for Grade 4 Mathematics: multiple-choice, short-answer, and extended-response. The Mathematics test includes approximately 32 multiple-choice items, 6 short-answer items (at least one for each content standard category), and 2 extended-response items.

Multiple-Choice Items

Multiple-choice items require you to select the correct response from a list of four choices. Each multiple-choice item is worth one point.

Short-Answer and Extended-Response Items

A short-answer item requires you to generate a written response. A short-answer requires a brief response, usually a word, a phrase, a sentence, or a numeric solution to a straightforward problem. A short-answer item may take up to five minutes to complete, and you will receive a score of 0, 1, or 2 points per test item. There is no penalty for guessing; an item without a response will automatically be counted as incorrect.

An extended-response item requires you to generate a written response. An extended-response item requires you to solve a more complex problem or task and to provide a more in-depth response. You are typically asked to show your work or calculations, explain your reasoning, and justify the procedure used. An extended-response item may require 5 to 15 minutes to complete, and responses receive a score of 0, 1, 2, 3, or 4 points per item. Below are samples of how short-answer and extended-response test items are scored.

Short-Answer Scoring Rubric

2-points
- Shows complete understanding of the concept or task
- Shows logical reasoning and conclusions
- Shows correct setup and/or computations

1-point
- Contains minor flaws in reasoning
- Neglects to address some aspect of the task or contains a computational error

Zero (0)
- Indicates no mathematical understanding of the concept or task

Extended-Response Scoring Rubric

4-points
- Contains an effective solution
- Shows complete understanding of the concept or task
- Addresses thoroughly the points relevant to the solution
- Contains logical reasoning and valid conclusions
- Communicates effectively and clearly through writing and/or diagrams
- Includes adequate and correct computations and/or setup when required

3-points
- Contains minor flaws
- Indicates an understanding of the concept or task
- Communicates adequately through writing and/or diagrams
- Reaches generally reasonable conclusions
- Contains minor flaws in reasoning and/or computation, or neglects to address some aspect of the item

2-points
- Indicates gaps in understanding and/or execution
- Contains some combination of the following flaws: an incomplete understanding of the concept or item, failure to address some points relevant to the solution, faulty reasoning, weak conclusions, unclear communication in writing and/or diagrams, a poor understanding of relevant mathematical procedures or concepts

1-point
- Indicates some effort beyond restating the item or copying given data
- Contains some combination of the following flaws: little understanding of the concept or item, failure to address most aspects of the item or solution, major flaws in reasoning that led to invalid conclusions, a definite lack of understanding of relevant mathematical procedures or concepts, omission of significant parts of the item and solution or response

Zero (0)
- Indicates no mathematical understanding of the concept or task

Directions for Practice Test 1

This Grade 4 Mathematics Achievement Practice Test has 40 multiple-choice, short-answer, and extended-response questions.

There are several important things to remember as you take this test:
- Read each multiple-choice question carefully. Think about what is being asked. Then fill in one answer bubble to mark your answer.
- If you do not know the answer to a multiple-choice question, skip it and go on. If you have time, go back to the questions you skipped and answer them.
- For short-answer and extended-response questions, write your response clearly and neatly on the lines provided.
- If you finish the Practice Test early, go back and check over your work.

1. Jainie rolls 5 dice. She rolls the following numbers: 1, 3, 5, 5, 6. What is the greatest number Jainie can make using these numbers and placing a 6 in the tens place?

   ○ A. 65,531
   ○ B. 55,163
   ○ C. 55,361
   ○ D. 5,361

2. For a math project, the students in Mr. Yamato's class were asked to find how old they were in days. The ages of four of his students are given in the table below. Which of the following lists the students from the oldest to the youngest?

Name	Age (in days)
Harry	3,698
Kendra	3,721
Mike	3,629
Marta	3,709

   ○ A. Marta, Kendra, Harry, Mike
   ○ B. Kendra, Marta, Harry, Mike
   ○ C. Marta, Kendra, Mike, Harry
   ○ D. Kendra, Marta, Mike, Harry

3. The models below are shaded to show that

   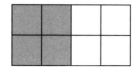 

   ○ A. $\frac{1}{4} = \frac{1}{2}$
   ○ B. $\frac{1}{4} < \frac{1}{2}$
   ○ C. $\frac{4}{8} > \frac{1}{2}$
   ○ D. $\frac{4}{8} = \frac{1}{2}$

4. Look at the model. Which fraction is shown by the model?

   ○ A. $\frac{5}{2}$
   ○ B. $\frac{5}{6}$
   ○ C. $\frac{3}{2}$
   ○ D. $\frac{3}{6}$

Go to next page

5. Look at the model. Which decimal is shown by the model?

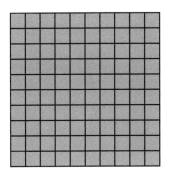 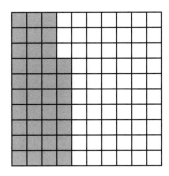

○ A. 0.37
○ B. 1.37
○ C. 1.63
○ D. 2.37

6. Brittany decided to surprise her mother by gluing a lace cord around the front cover of her address book. The address book is 8 inches tall and 6 inches wide. How much lace cord will Brittany need to go around the front cover of the book?

○ A. 48 inches
○ B. 28 inches
○ C. 14 square inches
○ D. 48 square inches

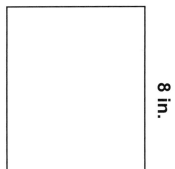

7. The two fourth-grade classes at Juniper Elementary School were having a recycling contest. Each class brought in aluminum cans to recycle. Mr. Loman's class brought in a total of 1,731 cans. Mrs. Inguagiato's class brought in a total of 1,588 cans. How many more cans did Mr. Loman's class bring in for the contest?

○ A. 43 cans
○ B. 53 cans
○ C. 143 cans
○ D. 153 cans

Go to next page

8. $1.31 - 0.89 =$

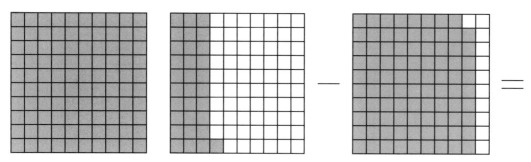

- A. 2.2
- B. 1.2
- C. 0.52
- D. 0.42

9. Polly has her books on some shelves in her room. Which number sentence represents the number of books Polly has as shown in the picture below?

- A. 4 x 7 = 28
- B. 4 x 8 = 32
- C. 4 + 8 = 12
- D. 8 + 8 = 16

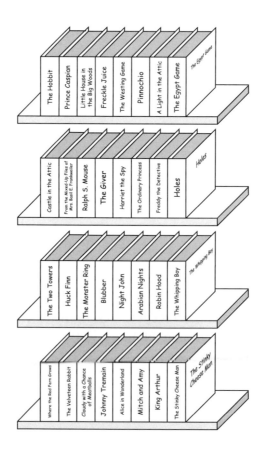

10. Which number sentence is true if a 6 is placed in the box?

    ○ A. 9 x ☐ = 54
    ○ B. 6 x ☐ = 12
    ○ C. 8 x ☐ = 42
    ○ D. 12 x ☐ = 18

11. Becca and Stephanie were selling tickets for a raffle. Becca sold 1,322 tickets. Stephanie sold 1,537 tickets. Which is the best estimate of the total number of tickets Becca and Stephanie sold?

    ○ A. 2,000 tickets
    ○ B. 2,700 tickets
    ○ C. 2,800 tickets
    ○ D. 3,200 tickets

12 What number completes the following number sentence?

    ☐ + 3 = 14

    _____

    _____

13. Wilbur is making popcorn for his class. He needs to make 8 cups of popcorn. The popcorn jar has the following table on the back to show about how many kernels are in certain measurements. How many kernels will Wilbur use to make 8 cups of popcorn?

Cups	1	2	3	4
Kernels	100	200	300	400

   ○ A. 700 kernels
   ○ B. 800 kernels
   ○ C. 900 kernels
   ○ D. 1,000 kernels

14. Ms. Lightfoot's science class is studying rocks. She asks each of her 24 students to collect 10 rocks. The table below shows how many rocks there are for a certain number of students. How many rocks did the entire class collect?

Students	1	3	7	8	13
Rocks	10	30	70	80	130

- A. 240 rocks
- B. 200 rocks
- C. 140 rocks
- D. 34 rocks

15. Fred works at a berry farm. He picks the berries and puts them in baskets. Each basket he fills must have exactly 25 berries in it. The table below shows this information. What number is missing from the table?

Baskets	1	3	6	8
Berries	25	75	?	200

- A. 100
- B. 125
- C. 150
- D. 175

16. At Coaster King amusement park, the most popular ride is the Electric Carrot. Each coaster train on the Electric Carrot holds 32 people. The table below shows this information. What number is missing from the table?

Number of Coaster Trains	1	2	4	6	8
People	32	64	128	?	256

- A. 256
- B. 160
- C. 224
- D. 192

Go to next page

17. Which pair of lines best represents perpendicular lines?

   ○ A.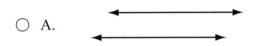

   ○ B.

   ○ C.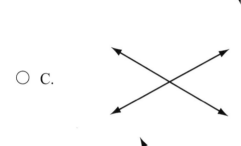

   ○ D.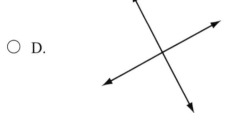

19. Which of the following figures is NOT congruent to the other 3 figures?

   ○ A.

   ○ B.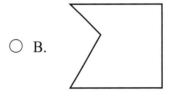

   ○ C.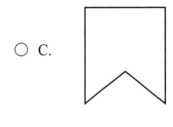

   ○ D.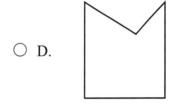

18. Which of the solids named below has exactly 5 vertices?

   ○ A. square pyramid

   ○ B. cube

   ○ C. triangular prism

   ○ D. sphere

20. Which pair of figures is congruent?

○ A.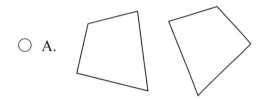

○ B.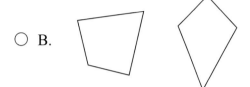

○ C.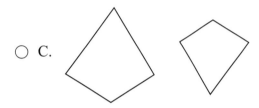

○ D.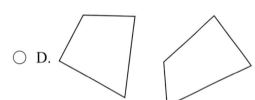

21. Which pair of figures below shows a reflection?

○ A.

○ B.

○ C.

○ D.

22. The grid below shows the size of Jasmine's room. Her bed is shown in the room. What is the area of Jasmine's bed?

○ A. 20 square feet
○ B. 22 square feet
○ C. 30 square feet
○ D. 96 square feet

Go to next page ➡

23. Caleb has a bag of 8 marbles. He has 3 red marbles, 2 green marbles, 1 silver marble, 1 purple marble, and 1 blue marble. If he takes 1 marble from the bag without looking, what is the probability that he will pick a green marble?

○ A. 2 out of 8
○ B. 6 out of 8
○ C. 2 out of 6
○ D. 6 out of 6

24. Mr. Moriarty's class was taking a survey of fourth graders' favorite kinds of pizza. They asked each fourth-grade student to choose his or her favorite kind of pizza. They recorded the results in the bar graph below. According to the bar graph, how many students are in the fourth grade?

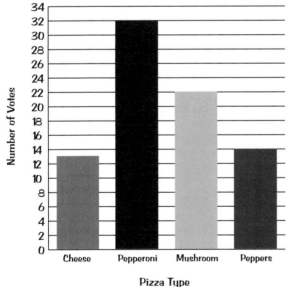

25. Last April, it rained twice as much as it had rained in March. This month, it rained one-fourth as much as it had rained in April. Which of the following statements is true?

○ A. It rained more in March than in April.
○ B. It rained less this month than in March.
○ C. It rained more this month than in April.
○ D. It rained less in March than in this month.

26. The four fourth-grade classes at Frank Elementary School were taking a survey to find what holiday students like best. They recorded their results in the bar graph below. Reggie looked at the graph below and made the generalization that "the students of Mr. Wysocki's class like Halloween better than Thanksgiving."

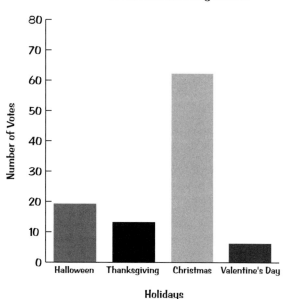

Which of the following statements uses information from the graph to either support this or show it is an incorrect statement?

○ A. The bar showing the votes for Halloween is larger than the bar showing the votes for Thanksgiving.

○ B. The bar showing the votes for Thanksgiving is larger than the bar showing the votes for Halloween.

○ C. The students should not have used a bar graph to show the results.

○ D. The bar graph does not show votes for Mr. Wysocki's class only. The graph is for the entire fourth grade.

27. The table below shows the number of pencils each person has in his or her collection, from Shania, who has the least number of pencils, to Pepe, who has the greatest number of pencils. Which of the following statements could NOT describe the number of pencils in Carolyn's collection?

Name	Pencils
Shania	86
Ralph	103
Carolyn	?
Mark	?
Elaine	187
Pepe	205

○ A. greater than 102 pencils

○ B. between 103 and 156 pencils

○ C. between 119 and 187 pencils

○ D. less than 103 pencils

28. Mrs. Pawlecki's class made a chart of the high and low temperatures every day for a week. That chart is shown below. At the end of the week, they made the generalization that it was warmer than 67° F at some point on each day during the week. Which of the following statements supports this generalization?

Day	High	Low
Sunday	73°F	66°F
Monday	75°F	65°F
Tuesday	80°F	69°F
Wednesday	83°F	70°F
Thursday	74°F	62°F
Friday	68°F	59°F
Saturday	70°F	63°F

○ A. The greatest of the low temperatures during the week was 70°F.

○ B. The lowest of the high temperatures during the week was 68°F.

○ C. The highest temperature during the week was 83°F.

○ D. The lowest temperature during the week was 59°F.

29. A garden in the shape of a rectangle is 10 feet wide and 15 feet long. What is the perimeter of the garden? Mark your answer.

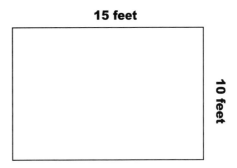

○ A. 20 feet

○ B. 25 feet

○ C. 30 feet

○ D. 50 feet

30. Sarah knows that water freezes at 32°F. The thermometer below shows the temperature outside. How much does the temperature need to change so water will freeze?

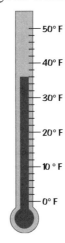

○ A. The temperature needs to go up 4°F.

○ B. The temperature needs to go up 2°F.

○ C. The temperature needs to go down 2°F.

○ D. The temperature needs to go down 4°F.

Go to next page

31. Mr. Kahn has a rectangular swimming pool, as shown below. How would Mr. Kahn find the perimeter of his pool? Mark your answer.

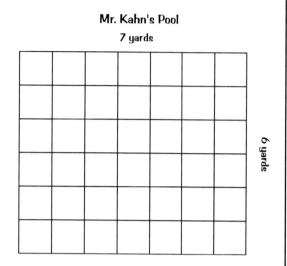

- A. Add 7 yards, 7 yards, 6 yards, and 6 yards.
- B. Add 7 yards and 6 yards.
- C. Multiply 7 yards and 6 yards.
- D. Multiply 7 yards, 7 yards, 6 yards, and 6 yards.

32. The thermometers below show the temperatures on Wednesday and Thursday. How many degrees did the temperature drop from Wednesday to Thursday?

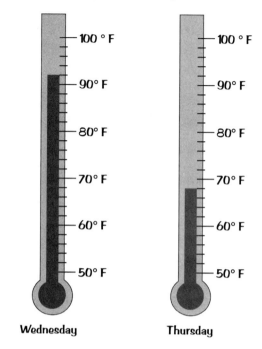

_____

_____

33. Ten students took Mr. Moore's math test on Friday. Their scores are listed below. What is the median of this set of scores?

68, 80, 80, 80, 83, 83, 89, 93, 95, 99

- A. 78
- B. 85
- C. 83
- D. 80

34. Use the map below to answer the following question.

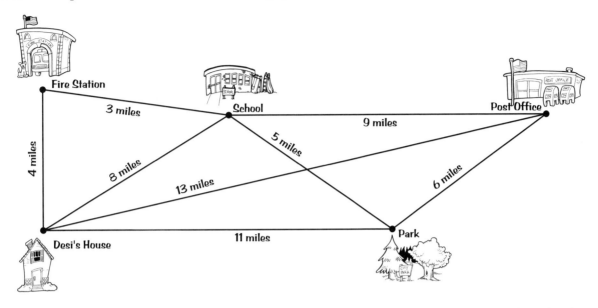

Desi would like to travel to all of the places shown on the map of her community, but she doesn't want to travel more than 24 miles total today. Name all of the places Desi can go today without traveling more than 24 miles. How many miles will Desi have traveled on the route you described? Remember, Desi must begin and end at her house.

_____

_____

_____

_____

35. Find the missing number and the rule for the pattern in the table below.

4	11	5	9	3
16	44	20	36	?

_____

_____

36. On the section of ruler shown below, the lines that are used to measure are

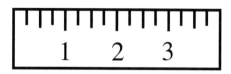

○ A. perpendicular to each other.

○ B. intersecting.

○ C. parallel to each other.

○ D. perpendicular, but not intersecting.

37. Marcos bought a DVD for $15.89. He gave the salesperson a twenty-dollar bill. Draw a picture to show the amount of money he should receive back. Explain your answer.

38. Name the two-dimensional shapes that make up the faces of the prism below. Tell how many faces there are of each shape.

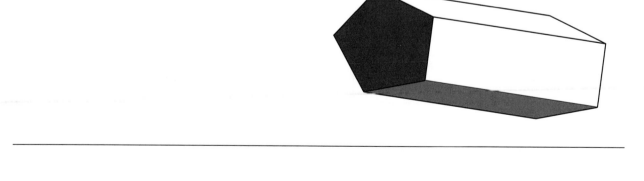

39. Wycliff, Clifford, and Sebastian competed in the school's annual triathlon. They competed in running, cycling, and swimming events. All three sports were timed, and the person with the lowest combined time was the Grand Prize Winner. Use the information in the table below to determine the Grand Prize Winner.

Events	Wycliff	Clifford	Sebastian
Running	4.1 min.	4.4 min	4.6 min.
Cycling	7.3 min.	7.4 min.	6.8 min.
Swimming	5.0 min.	5.0 min.	4.9 min.

○ A. The Grand Prize winner was Wycliff.

○ B. The Grand Prize winner was Clifford.

○ C. The Grand Prize winner was Sebastian.

○ D. The Grand Prize winners were Sebastian and Wycliff, who had the same combined time.

40. What is the area of the irregular shape below?

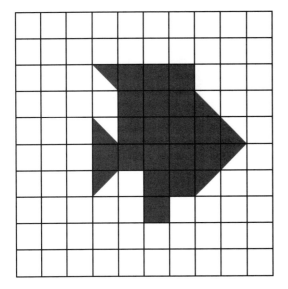

○ A. 24.5 squares

○ B. 21.5 squares

○ C. 20 squares

○ D. 23 squares

Directions for Practice Test 2

This Grade 4 Mathematics Achievement Practice Test has 40 multiple-choice, short-answer, and extended-response questions.

There are several important things to remember as you take this test:
- Read each multiple-choice question carefully. Think about what is being asked. Then fill in one answer bubble to mark your answer.
- If you do not know the answer to a multiple-choice question, skip it and go on. If you have time, go back to the questions you skipped and answer them.
- For short-answer and extended-response questions, write your response clearly and neatly on the lines provided.
- If you finish the Practice Test early, go back and check over your work.

1. The 2 circles are shaded to show that

   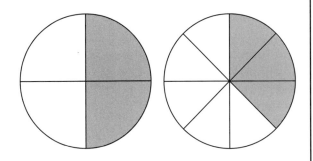

   ○ A. $\frac{3}{8} > \frac{2}{4}$

   ○ B. $\frac{2}{4} > \frac{3}{8}$

   ○ C. $\frac{2}{4} < \frac{3}{8}$

   ○ D. $\frac{2}{4} > \frac{5}{8}$

2. $0.71 + 0.53 =$

   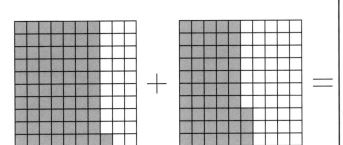

   ○ A. 0.18
   ○ B. 0.24
   ○ C. 1.18
   ○ D. 1.24

3. What is the missing factor in the number sentence representing the model shown below?

   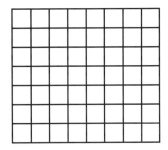

   8 x ___

   ○ A. 56
   ○ B. 30
   ○ C. 8
   ○ D. 7

4. Julio collects baseball cards. Each pack of baseball cards he buys has 12 cards in it. Write a number sentence to show how many baseball cards Julio will have if he buys 9 packs of baseball cards.

   _____

   _____

5. Ruth has a box of cookies she wants to share with her friends. The box has 54 cookies in it. Ruth and her 2 friends will each get the same number of cookies. How many cookies will the 3 friends each get?

   ○ A. 18 cookies
   ○ B. 24 cookies
   ○ C. 27 cookies
   ○ D. 51 cookies

   Go to next page ▶

6. A football player was signing autographs for his fans. He could sign 12 autographs in 1 minute. Which is the best estimate of the number of autographs the player could sign in 11 minutes?

   ○ A. 23 autographs
   ○ B. 75 autographs
   ○ C. 110 autographs
   ○ D. 180 autographs

7. A flock of 29 birds was flying south for the winter. They could fly 22 miles in 1 hour. Which is the best estimate of how many miles they could travel in 5 hours?

   ○ A. 600 miles
   ○ B. 300 miles
   ○ C. 150 miles
   ○ D. 100 miles

8. At the Chip-Off-the-Old-Block snack factory, bags of potato chips are packed in boxes. The table below shows how many bags of potato chips are packed. Which expression shows how to find the missing number?

Boxes	Bags
3	45
6	90
8	?
10	150

   ○ A. 150 ÷ 8
   ○ B. 8 x 15
   ○ C. 45 + 90
   ○ D. 150 – 15

9. Jeremy's mom left to drop him off at Eddie's house at 3:00. It takes 3 minutes to drive from Jeremy's house to the park. From the park to the library, it takes 8 minutes. It takes 4 minutes to get to Eddie's house from the library. If Jeremy's mom leaves right after dropping him off at Eddie's, at what time does she get home?

   ○ A. 3:15
   ○ B. 3:30
   ○ C. 3:45
   ○ D. 4:00

10. Mrs. McPherson's class and Mrs. Cellio's class took a field trip to the zoo. There are 29 students in Mrs. McPherson's class, and there are 26 students in Mrs. Cellio's class. The students were told to divide into groups of 4 students each, but there were not enough students to make even groups. How many students were left after the 2 classes were divided into groups of 4 students each?

    ○ A. 13 students
    ○ B. 3 students
    ○ C. 2 students
    ○ D. 1 student

11. Vidar had $19.00. He spent $3.00 on candy. The magazine he wanted cost half of what he had left. How can you find how much money Vidar spent on the magazine?

    ○ A. divide $19.00 by 2
    ○ B. subtract $3.00 from $16.00
    ○ C. add $3.00 to $8.00
    ○ D. divide $16.00 by 2

Go to next page ➡

12. Pedro is building a raft. His tools include a measuring tape and a saw. He has 5 logs that are each 6 feet long and 1 foot wide. He also has 30 feet of rope. To build his raft, he will lay the logs in a row and tie the rope around them in two places, as shown in the diagram below. He wants his raft to be a square. Which of the following statements is true?

○ A. Pedro can build his square raft without sawing off any wood.

○ B. Pedro cannot build his square raft without sawing off some wood.

○ C. Pedro cannot build his square raft because he needs more rope.

○ D. Pedro can build his square raft, but he only needs 20 feet of rope to do it.

13. A buckeye tree produced 47 buckeyes one year. Of those buckeyes, all but 19 were taken by animals. The next year, the same tree produced 53 buckeyes. Only 13 of those buckeyes were taken by animals. Write a number sentence that could be used to find how many buckeyes were NOT taken by animals in those two years.

_____

_____

14. Which of the following solids has the greatest number of faces?

○ A.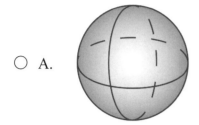

○ C.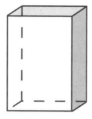

○ B.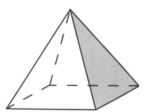

○ D.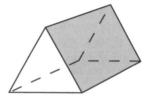

15. Mrs. Williams made a blanket for her grandson, David. The blanket is shown below. What is the area of the shaded squares of the blanket?

   ○ A. 3 square feet
   ○ B. 6 square feet
   ○ C. 12 square feet
   ○ D. 14 square feet

   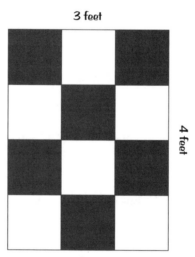

16. Henry hit 4 home runs in a baseball game. The distance the ball traveled for each home run is shown in the table below. What is the total distance of the home runs Henry hit?

   ○ A. 1,866 feet
   ○ B. 1,876 feet
   ○ C. 1,966 feet
   ○ D. 1,976 feet

Home Run	Distance
1st	457 ft.
2nd	513 ft.
3rd	429 ft.
4th	577 ft.

Go to next page

17. Gina is doing a puzzle. The puzzle has 1,225 pieces. The table below shows how many pieces she can put together in a certain amount of time. Which number sentence shows how Gina can find how many pieces she can put together in 5 minutes?

    ○ A. 52 + 39
    ○ B. 143 ÷ 11
    ○ C. 13 x 5
    ○ D. 91 − 52

Minutes	Pieces
3	39
4	52
5	?
7	91
11	143

18. According to the bar graph below, how many more students have brown eyes than have blue eyes?

    ○ A. 42
    ○ B. 38
    ○ C. 26
    ○ D. 18

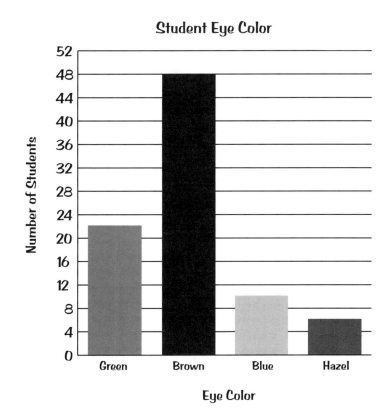

19. Each wall in the art museum has the same number of paintings on it. This is shown in the table below. What number is missing from the table?

Walls	Paintings
3	21
5	35
6	42
8	56
12	?

○ A. 84

○ B. 70

○ C. 63

○ D. 77

20. Rudy and her 2 younger brothers each built a snowman. Which of the following statements is true about the snowmen they built?

○ A. All the snowmen are the same height.

○ B. The snowman's hat is a cone.

○ C. Each snowman has a nose shaped like a circle.

○ D. The snowmen are not congruent to one another.

21. Lon, Bela, Boris, and Robert each had a full can of soda. Boris drank half of his soda. Lon drank half of what Boris had drunk. Bela drank 3 times as much as Lon had. Robert drank twice as much as Lon had drunk. Whose can of soda has the least amount of soda left in it?

    ○ A. Lon's
    ○ B. Bela's
    ○ C. Boris'
    ○ D. Robert's

22. Belle is playing a board game with her family. In the game, each time your piece touches a red space, you earn 100 points. Belle's brother's piece touches 5 red spaces in one turn, so he earns 500 points. Belle's mother earns 300 points for touching 3 red spaces with her piece in one turn. If Belle's piece touches 8 red spaces in one turn, how many points will she earn?

    ○ A. 200
    ○ B. 400
    ○ C. 500
    ○ D. 800

23. Dawn's frog, Sir Hops-A-Lot, grows in a pattern. How many ounces does Sir Hops-A-Lot gain in weight each time he grows an inch in length?

Weight	9 oz.	15 oz.	21 oz.	33 oz.
Length	3 in.	5 in.	7 in.	11 in.

    ○ A. 2 oz.
    ○ B. 3 oz.
    ○ C. 6 oz.
    ○ D. 8 oz.

24. Which of the following figures is NOT congruent to the others?

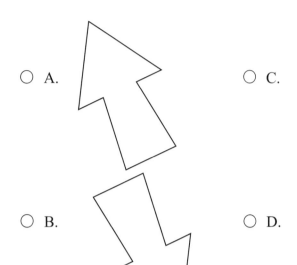

○ A.

○ B.

○ C.

○ D.

25. There are 5 people in the Marquez family. Anna was born in April. Lupe and George were both born in June. Angel was born in November. Pepe was born in December. If one of the Marquez family members was chosen at random, what is the probability that the person chosen will NOT have been born in June?

○ A. 1 out of 5

○ B. 2 out of 5

○ C. 3 out of 5

○ D. 4 out of 5

26. The bar graph below shows the number of shoes produced at a shoe factory from April to July. Which of the following statements is NOT supported by the graph?

○ A. More shoes were produced from June to July than from April to May.

○ B. The most shoes were produced in June.

○ C. At least 7,000 shoes were produced each month.

○ D. The total number of shoes produced from April to July is greater than 28,000 shoes.

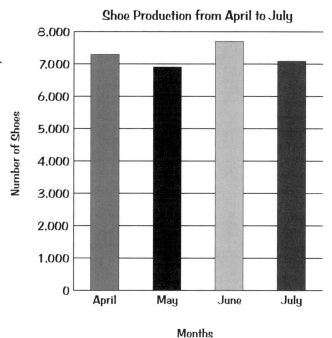

27. The bar graph below shows the number of flowers that bloomed in Flora's garden over the past 4 years. Only a third of the flowers she planted bloomed each year. What is the total number of flowers she planted from 2001 to 2002?

○ A. 234
○ B. 504
○ C. 384
○ D. 270

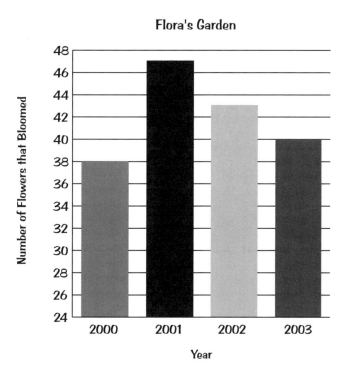

Go to next page

28. What is the area of the flag below in square units? Mark your answer.

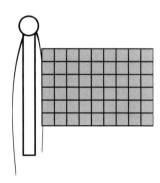

○ A. 58 square units
○ B. 54 square units
○ C. 48 square units
○ D. 44 square units

29. Roberto has a set of flash cards. One flash card is shown below. He put 9 of the cards end to end across the top of a small table. There were 2 more inches from the end of the last card to the edge of the table. What is the total length of the table in inches?

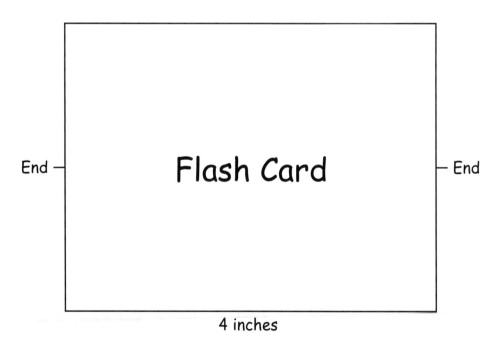

○ A. 36 inches
○ B. 38 inches
○ C. 6 inches
○ D. 34 inches

30. Paco was in charge of bringing candy to the class Halloween party. He bought 3 bags of candy. One bag had 372 pieces of candy. Another bag had 157 pieces of candy. The third bag had 284 pieces of candy. What is the total number of pieces of candy Paco bought?

_____

_____

31. What are the chances of spinning an odd number using the spinner shown?

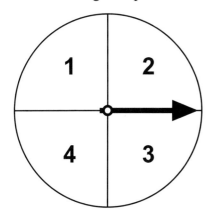

A. $\dfrac{1}{4}$

B. $\dfrac{2}{4}$

C. $\dfrac{0}{4}$

D. $\dfrac{4}{4}$

32. What type of figures are shown below?

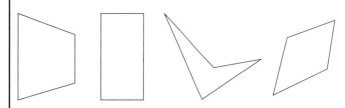

○ A. quadrillaterals

○ B. squares

○ C. triangles

○ D. parallelograms

33. If the number that would come next in the pattern below is 28, what is the rule of the pattern?

4, 8, 12, 16, 20, 24, ____

○ A. add 4

○ B. multiply by 2

○ C. divide by 4

○ D. multiply by 2, then subtract 1

34. Of the figures shown below, which one is not congruent with the others and why?

A   B   C   D

_____

_____

_____

Go to next page ➡

35. Examine the two shapes shown below. Explain how they are alike and how they are different.

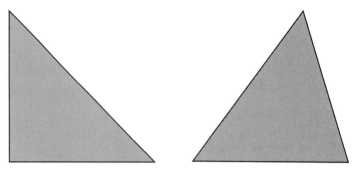

_____
_____
_____
_____

36. Ashley's Girl Scout troop sold cookies at a fund-raiser. Ashley sold 20 boxes of cookies. Her friend Krista sold 15 more boxes than Ashley sold. Which equation should be used to find how many boxes Krista sold?

   ○ A. $20 + 15 = n$
   ○ B. $20 - n = 15$
   ○ C. $15 + n = 20$
   ○ D. $20 - 15 = n$

37. On Monday morning, there were 13 baseballs signed by Omar Vizquel in a display. By Friday evening, 6 had been sold. Write a number sentence that could be used to find the number of baseballs remaining in the display.

_____
_____

38. Jordan was helping his parents prepare a sale display for their sporting goods store. First he needed to paint the background of the display board. The board was 5 feet long and 3 feet tall. What is the area of the display board? Write a number sentence that could be used to find the area of the display board.

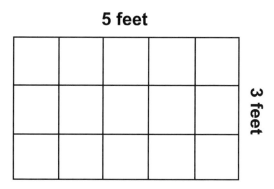

39. At the local swim meet, Sarah's swim time for Meet 3 was 56.9 seconds. Angela's time on the same event was 57.03 seconds. Enter their times in the table shown. Based upon the scores for the first three meets shown in the table, who will most likely win the 100-yard backstroke in Meet 4?

Event: 100-yard backstroke

SWIMMER	MEET 1	MEET 2	MEET 3
Jamie	57.00	57.01	57.08
Angela	57.03	57.10	
Doris	58.11	58.09	58.00
Sarah	56.89	56.91	

Go to next page

40. Letters A, B, C, D, and E are on the other side of the cards shown. The chance of turning over the letter M is

○ A. $\frac{1}{2}$

○ B. $\frac{1}{5}$

○ C. 0

○ D. 1

Thank YOU For Your Purchase!

For more information on our OAT products call 1-877-PASSING (727-7464), or visit our website:

www.passtheoat.com